GOLD MEDAL DIARY

GOLD

HAYLEY WICKENHEISER

MEDAL DIARY

INSIDE THE WORLD'S

GREATEST SPORTS EVENT

GREYSTONE BOOKS

D&M PUBLISHERS INC.

Vancouver/Toronto/Berkeley

Greystone Books
An imprint of D&M Publishers Inc.
2323 Quebec Street, Suite 201
Vancouver BC Canada V5T 4S7
www.greystonebooks.com

Cataloguing data available from Library and Archives Canada

ISBN 978-1-55365-580-0 (cloth)   ISBN 978-1-55365-595-4 (ebook)

Editing by Peter Norman
Jacket design by Naomi MacDougall
Text design by Heather Pringle
Jacket photograph © Bruce Bennett/Getty Images
Printed and bound in Canada by Friesens
Text printed on acid-free, 100% post-consumer paper
Distributed in the U.S. by Publishers Group West

We gratefully acknowledge the financial support of the Canada Council for the Arts,
the British Columbia Arts Council, the Province of British Columbia through the
Book Publishing Tax Credit, and the Government of Canada through the Canada
Book Fund for our publishing activities.

For Noah,
who keeps my feet on the ground . . .
and to all the women who paved the way
long before I played the game, thank you.
This book is for you.

And special thanks to Wendy Long,
for her passion and commitment
in making this book possible.

INTRODUCTION

by Wendy Long

USA 4, CANADA 1

The final score from the 2009 Women's World Ice Hockey Championship was hardly the result the Canadian women's team wanted just ten months from the 2010 Olympic Winter Games in Vancouver. Indeed, if there was anything more galling than the loss in the tournament final in Finland, it was knowing the result marked the second consecutive world title for the Americans after they edged Team Canada 4–3 in the 2008 championship final.

In sport, dwelling on the past can be as dangerous as resting on laurels. Few players understood those pitfalls better than Canadian team captain Hayley Wickenheiser.

She was just nineteen when Team Canada was favoured heavily to win gold at the 1998 Winter Olympics in Nagano. But it was the United States who made history as the inaugural Olympic women's hockey champion, defeating four-time world champion Canada 7–4 in the round robin, then prevailing 3–1 in the final.

Expectation is a precarious thing, particularly in sport, where the unbidden has been the undoing of many a favoured team or athlete. The Canadians returned from Nagano with silver medals and lessons learned about competing in an Olympic atmosphere that boils with hype and assumption. The importance of staying grounded—seeing to small details while refusing to allow sport's highs and lows to take control—resonated with Wickenheiser. She moved on from the Nagano experience to become one of Canada's most recognized athletes, regarded as the finest woman hockey player in the world.

She was born in Shaunavon, Saskatchewan, blessed with an athletic prowess that led her to excel in many sports. She developed a passion for hockey, despite a dearth of hockey programs and opportunities for girls. No problem. She played on boys' hockey teams. In the summer, she honed her skills on the softball diamond.

At fifteen, having earlier moved to Calgary with her family, Wickenheiser was named to the national women's hockey team, and in 1994 she played in her first world championship. She earned one assist in three games as her team won its third consecutive world title. Four years later, Nagano marked her Winter Olympic debut and, after those Games, Philadelphia Flyers general manager Bobby Clarke invited her to his team's rookie camp later in the year. In 2000 she exchanged her hockey stick for a bat and competed in the Summer Olympics in Sydney as a member of the Canadian women's softball team.

Her athleticism, skill, and passion for hockey earned a host of accolades. At the 2001 Canadian Sport Awards she was honoured with the Bruce Kidd Award for athletic leadership. Wickenheiser went on to become top scorer and named most valuable player at the 2002 and 2006 Olympic women's tournaments, leading Canada to gold medal victories at both Games. In 2007 she took home the Bobbie Rosenfeld Award as the Canadian Press female athlete of the year. A year later she was number twenty on *Sports Illustrated*'s list of 25 Toughest Athletes.

Add "trailblazer" to the Wickenheiser list of attributes, which also includes goal scorer, playmaker, and role model. In the fall of 2002 she embarked on a remarkable hockey journey, playing professional men's hockey in Finland with HC Salamat. In January

2003 she became the first woman to score a goal in a men's professional hockey league and helped her team earn promotion to a higher division the following season.

Five years later Wickenheiser travelled to Sweden with her partner, Tomas Pacina, and son, Noah, to compete in the men's professional ranks. She played the 2008–2009 season with third-division men's team Eskilstuna Linden.

On July 2, 2003, International Olympic Committee president Jacques Rogge announced that Vancouver had won the right to play host to the 2010 Olympic Winter Games. Amidst the jubilation it was already clear that Canadians, who had relished their men's and women's teams winning hockey gold in Salt Lake City a year earlier, would have high expectations for their hockey teams at the home Games in Vancouver. Hockey is, after all, a national pastime— if not a national obsession.

Canada had last played host to the Olympics in Calgary in 1988. Who would step up and make the host nation proud in 2010? Hopes ran high for the country's athletes in all sports, but Canadian hockey players shouldered the greatest share of the expectation burden. Olympic hockey gold for Canada, in Canada, was not an option. It was a requirement.

So it was that the twenty-first Olympic Winter Games opened in Vancouver on a rainy, west coast February night brimming with celebration and anticipation...

FEBRUARY 12, 2010

I will never forget this day. Amazing. Amazing! Where do I start?

Today Canada welcomed the world, and we marched in as the host nation team at the opening ceremonies of the Vancouver Olympic Winter Games. The athletes here have spent almost four years preparing for the competition that will unfold over the next two weeks. The opening ceremonies honour these athletes, who have come together in the spirit of sport and competition. There is nothing quite like walking into a stadium for an opening ceremonies and feeling the joy, optimism, and enthusiasm in the parade of athletes.

Not every competitor takes part in the ceremonies. Some have yet to arrive in Vancouver as their events may not begin for another week. Some compete tomorrow and are taking time to focus and prepare. Our Canadian women's hockey team plays Slovakia tomorrow, but we all chose to take part in the ceremonies. None of us wanted to miss out on the Olympic experience. It starts with the opening ceremonies, where as an athlete you connect with the rest of the world—you become immersed in not only community spirit but a world spirit.

OUR DAY BEGAN WITH practice on the fresh Olympic ice at GM Place, or Canada Hockey Place, as it's called for these Games. We watched

Slovakia practise before we went on the ice. They didn't look very good. They're pretty big and seem to have decent goaltending, but that's about it. I think it's going to be a tough game for them tomorrow.

Afterward I walked around the waterfront to Science World, which during the Games is the official pavilion of Sochi, Russia, host of the 2014 Winter Games. There I met Mom, Dad, Noah, my best friend, Danielle Greenberg, and Syl Corbett, my sport thera- pist. It was so great to see them. It was raining, and Noah didn't want to wear his poncho, and he was cranky because his flight from Calgary got in late the night before. We went to Starbucks. I was a little tight after practice, so Syl gave me a treatment right there, which was quite funny. There I was, lying on a piece of newspaper on the floor of the Starbucks, while she was tweaking me, flexing my legs, and all sorts of things. The things you do at the Olympics!

If I go out in public now, I need to wear regular clothes, and probably a hat, because as soon as people see the team jacket or athlete accreditation they want to come up and say hi. There are lots of well-wishers and picture-takers. If I don't want to have that attention I definitely need to go incognito, which I learned just from hanging out in that Starbucks.

I started to feel a little stressed after I returned to the village. I wanted to fix my hair and put some makeup on because soon I was going to be in front of the world, three billion people. These are moments that live with you forever and you want to take advan- tage of them as best as you can. I took an hour to get ready. I put on my TV makeup because, well, I guess I had some experience with that at the Summer Games in Beijing, doing colour commentary for softball. I wanted to look my best. My roomies, though, were wondering what was up because I usually take all of five minutes to get ready!

I put on our Team Canada Olympic ceremony clothing—a nice big parka with a scarf, and cords tucked into military-style boots.

Oh yes, and a toque. I really like the look. The Canadian team is going to look sharp. My roommates and I took pictures of one another in our gear, and then we were on our way.

WE GRABBED A QUICK quite bite to eat then met at 2:45 PM in the lobby of Canada House to go to Athlete Staging, which they did a little different this time around. At past Olympics they would have put us in the hockey arena at the same time as the rest of the world, about three hours before the ceremony. Instead, we had our own pep rally. There were speeches and videos—the "I Believe" videos—and messages from Sarah McLachlan, Steve Nash, Kim Cattrall. Also in attendance were Steve Podborski, Joé Juneau, Nathalie Lambert, Clara Hughes, Mark Tewksbury, and Julie Payette—they all spoke to us.

Joé Juneau's speech resonated with me, as it was very passionate. Using the image of the Inukshuk—the Inuit stone marker depicted in the official logo of the Vancouver Olympics—he explained that we athletes can be Inukshuk for kids watching us across the country and around the world. We can show the way. We can serve as signposts, or role models, for a way of life, a path of striving for excellence.

Mark Tewksbury was hilarious. He did a cheer that went like this: "I'm a beaver, you're a beaver, we're a beaver, ALL. And when we get together, we do the beaver CALL." What followed was a funny, stupid cheer. But it was also full of passion and emotion. And then he said, "Why not you? Why not you? Make it happen. This is your time. Time for you to shine and do what you need to do." Then he talked about his experience in Barcelona, where he won a gold medal in the backstroke final.

Steve Podborski talked about being injured and having to watching the Olympics, then coming back and competing. Nathalie Lambert, the chef de mission, talked about just enjoying the experience, being proud to be a Canadian.

Julie Payette talked about going into space, how her Olympics was getting to blast off into the atmosphere, and all the things she had done to get there. She mentioned the shirt that she took up there—it was signed by Canadian athletes, and it orbited the world 280 times.

The environment gave us an opportunity to rest and relax. It was certainly better than at other Olympics I have attended. Marnie McBean, manager of Olympic preparation for the Canadian team, also spoke. She recommended everybody walk into the stadium with no cameras, to just enjoy the moment. There was a lot of energy and excitement. All of us wondered what the world was going to see and what it would feel like to walk into the stadium as Canada's Olympic team.

We were herded into buses, went over to GM Place, and sat there for about forty-five minutes. They gave us a little snack pack— sesame seeds and cranberries and lots of water. It was important for us to sit down, to keep off our feet, because it was going to be a long night, and with a game the next day the last thing we needed was to have tired legs.

The HBC fashion police showed up, telling us how to wear the scarf that goes with the opening ceremony garb. No one was sure if it should be tucked in, wrapped around the neck, or if the jacket should be open or closed. It was kind of a gong show. But we got it all figured out. They wanted us to look just right. All this time I just sat there with the girls from the team, and chatted with some of the other athletes.

Eventually, the last team in front of us left GM Place. We got up and started walking across the street to B.C. Place. Nathalie Lambert had said earlier she would let people know if they were walking in the first two rows. Well, she came up to me and said, "Hayley, we'd like you to walk with us in the first row." I said, "Sure, I'd be honoured!" They had our goalie, Kim St-Pierre, walk in the second row. This is her third Olympics, and she has been one of the best goalies in the world. She has single-handedly won us many games over the years so the honour was well deserved.

I walked beside Joé Juneau, Jeremy Wotherspoon, Steve Podborski, Nathalie Lambert, and Pierre Lueders. Leading us all was our flag-bearer, Clara Hughes. The rest of our hockey team was supposed to walk behind us, but they went at the end to have more space.

We stood together and chatted, waiting to go in, wondering which team was currently walking into the stadium. I talked with Joé Juneau about how he handled pressure, how to perform and just hockey talk. I talked with Pierre Lueders, asking if it was going to be his last Games.

At one point I sat on the floor, up against the concrete wall, next to Clara Hughes and Chandra Crawford. About every ten minutes we moved a little bit. The blue-clad volunteers lining the hold were screaming and yelling "Way To Go, Canada" and taking pictures. It was a pretty cool thing, just to see how passionate people were, knowing they were all Canadian, feeling that wave of energy.

Inside, the athlete procession continued. Olympic tradition dictates that Greece, host of the first Olympics, always leads the parade of athletes, while the host country's team is the last to enter the stadium. Finally, they brought us to the tunnel. It was extremely hot inside that stadium, and by the time we moved into the close confines of the tunnel we were absolutely boiling. As we moved along, I was texting with Danielle, Noah, Syl, and a couple of people back home. I was asking, "How are things looking?" They were saying it was awesome. Clara, in front, looked fantastic as she took those first steps from the tunnel and led us into the stadium. We were engulfed in an indescribable roar. All we could see was white—the spectators were wearing white ponchos.

To walk in the stadium, to feel the crowd and the sound, was unbelievable. I wanted to soak it all in, receive that energy, feel what was happening in the stadium. I looked briefly for Mom and

Dad and the others, but I couldn't see them. I couldn't see faces, only a wall of white. To be walking with my fellow athletes, hand in hand, representing Canada, was truly incredible.

It was probably the fastest stadium lap of my life. I wanted it to last forever. The lap of an indoor stadium isn't very long—in Torino and other outdoor stadiums, it was a full four hundred metres. But inside B.C. Place, it was really short. The floor was made of white felt or foam. The stage looked magnificent. I thought we looked great as a Canadian team.

All too soon we arrived at our seats. I sat on the end so that it would be easy for me to get out. Joé Juneau sat beside me. I watched for about fifteen minutes, and then a handler came and took Michel Verrault and me to the green room. Sarah McLachlan had just finished performing. She was standing there—I tapped her back and said, "Way to go, you were great!" I've always loved her music. I sat there with Michel; we each got our white cue card and continued to watch the show—Garou, Loreena McKennitt, and a steady stream of people were coming in and out. I don't know how long I waited, probably forty-five minutes. Then I put my jacket on and the makeup people came over to administer a touch-up.

I rehearsed my lines for the athletes' oath. I felt calm. Opera singer Measha Brueggergosman came in, with her big hair, and I was struck by just how composed these performers are. I'm sure they get nervous and they focus in their own way. But they are so at ease with what they do, just as I am when I get out on the ice. I took a page out of their book and thought, "You know what? Screw it. I'm going to go out there in front of three billion people and do the best that I can, and be at ease. There's nothing to be nervous about."

Everyone on the stage, and everyone who marched in wearing a national team uniform, was there because they earned the right to be there, because they are very, very good at what they do.

Musicians, singers, entertainers, athletes—each in his or her own way has practised, persevered, and prevailed to achieve success. So much of performance, be it athletic or artistic, is about preparation, the daily grind of work and practice that sets a foundation for future success. You don't get here on hope or a wing and a prayer. As an athlete you get to the Olympics because you are persistent, passionate, and committed to your sport, determined to be the best you can be while also helping your teammates to do the same.

Most of the time, it's not a glamorous process. Getting to the Olympic Games is a difficult road. Our Canadian women's hockey team can attest to that. We've come a long way since we gathered in Calgary last summer to begin preparing for these Games.

1

THE ROAD
TO THE RINGS

AUGUST 8, 2009

Today is our first day on the ice together as we begin this journey to the 2010 Winter Games. I've started on this Olympic road a few times now, and each experience is different. I was thinking about it driving to the rink today and was struck that this time I don't feel too nervous, too anxious. Should I? Am I too comfortable, too settled? Should I be scaring myself? Keeping myself on edge? Having gone through these processes over the years, I've learned every day will not be the best. I just have to plug through the tough days. I never feel I'm ready, I feel there are still a million things to do.

Twenty-six players from across Canada are here, each hoping to earn one of twenty-one spots on the Olympic team roster. Our schedule from now until February is hectic. We have two international tournaments, a six-game series against the Americans, and about sixty other games slated against a variety of Midget AAA boys' teams. Five players will be cut at various points in this schedule. A few weeks ago, prior to this team centralization in Calgary, we also had a thirty-two-day conditioning camp in Dawson Creek. Training for the Olympics is, at this point, a full-time commitment. From experience I know that sometimes there will not seem to be enough hours in a day. Having the Olympics in Canada is sure to produce even more expectations and duties than normal for our team.

WE STARTED AT 9:30 AM today with a workout in the weight room. I was pretty bagged afterward, especially coming off a long summer of training with a lot of volume and intensity. But I had made it through the fitness testing with some personal bests, gains I had wanted to make that will carry over directly to the ice. Our head coach, Mel Davidson, writes a little bit about every day's practice on the chalkboard in the warm-up room; what to expect, what the goals are for the day.

Today the expectation was for good, crisp passes, puck protection, execution—all simple but important skills—so that we can move into more complex things. The game is about skills: passing, shooting, skating. Usually the team with the best execution of skills is the most successful. So the first couple of weeks here are just about skills. The schedule is also heavy with meetings and appointments with the team's sport psychologist, massage therapy, medical things to take care of... so many details.

Our first on-ice session was basically like hockey school. We did a lot of standing around, some puck protection drills. I had a new helmet that was squeezing my head so hard it felt like it was going to pop off. Time to get the legs going, to see how the body feels after the summer. This summer I was only on the ice for about three weeks because I knew we had a lot of games to play over the next seven months. I felt I needed to get away from the rink, work on my body, rebalance it, and get everything firing at top cylinder, with the help of Andy O'Brien, Kelsey Andries, and Syl Corbett— my little support team.

Andy has worked with Sidney Crosby since Crosby was thirteen. I met him when he worked as strength and fitness coach for the Florida Panthers, which Tomas also worked for. We've developed a good off-ice training routine, and this summer I focused on lateral strength and speed. It reflected in the team fitness testing: I made gains in agility, critical power, and speed endurance.

"Speed endurance" means that if you are at high speed you can find that next gear; coming out of a corner you make one or two quick steps and beat that guy or girl to the net. (I always talk in terms of "guys" because I've played with them for so long—guys or girls, it doesn't matter to me, they're just players.)

Kelsey is a strength and conditioning coach and a former free-style wrestler at the University of Calgary. She has helped me incorporate Andy's program into my daily routine, and she kicked my butt all summer.

Syl is a professional mountain runner and acts as my sport therapist, specializing in neural optimization, meaning she keeps me firing on all cylinders with a combination of stretches. She makes sure I have strength through range of motion.

Some days can really be a grind, but I take pride in taking care of my body. In this last off-season I put in a lot of time and effort to try to get better. You can't do these things without having a good support team around you. As you get older, you realize your body is your ticket and it's your machine. It takes a lot of time, energy, and money to take care of it. Thousands and thousands of dollars go into these things. That's why we are given our carding money—financial support to elite athletes that comes from the Sport Canada Athlete Assistance Program. We also rely on sponsors. For me, it's worth every cent to surround myself with the best people.

TEAM SWEDEN IS HERE. They will be playing our team and the under-22 players, who are also in town going through their selection process. We're scheduled to have four games against the under-22s and one against Sweden. I may not play every game, because we have twenty-six players, and twenty-one play in a game. So it will be an interesting few weeks, almost like a boot camp. We will probably be tired. The coaching staff doesn't care if we're tired or not at this point. They just want us to push through and get through these games leading into Vancouver and the Canada Cup at the end of the month.

Tomas and Noah are away for two weeks, so I'm by myself. This is good because I can focus, get myself on track when there are so many things that need attention. In our team meetings we've been talking about our value system, ironing out what our team values are going to be. What is professionalism? What is being a good teammate? What are our team values? In our program, the coaches often harp on doing the little things, daily habits. There's an expectation that when you play for Canada you carry on the tradition of excellence, the tradition of doing the right things. Young players who come into the system may not know these things. It's up to veterans like myself to demonstrate and live those values as an example for those who follow.

THE DAY FINISHED AT 5 PM. I came home, and Becky Kellar picked up a recliner and a couple of kids' toys for her rented house. I admire her. Her husband is back home in Burlington, and she brought her two kids and her mom and dad out here to live through the centralization process. It's not easy to relocate your entire life for six months but she handles it well. She's a very smart player and a smart person, and we need her.

After she left I cleaned up my house, organized Noah's Lego collection, did the laundry, made some dinner—chicken and steamed greens, couscous—ate, watched a bit of the news. I called Andy to talk about my training over the next couple of weeks. I sent some e-mails and took care of some business, organized my life for the next week. I made a list. I make lists every day so I can see what I didn't finish and what I need to do the next day. I cleaned up the clutter in my mind and in my life so that I can focus on what needs to be done.

By 9:15 PM I was ready to have a bath and read a bit of *The Metabolic Plan* by Stephen Cherniske. I don't really read for fun, because I don't have the time. I generally like to read things that can teach me something. Sometimes I fall asleep at night with my computer on, often I'll throw in a show or a movie just to knock me out. But I shouldn't have any problems tonight. Day one is done.

AUGUST 13

I need to go to bed—now! It's only 7:30 PM, but it's been a long day, a long couple of days. Yesterday was my birthday: I am now thirty-one years old. It's hard to believe I started playing on the national team when I was fifteen. I'm coming up to my fifth Olympic Games, including playing softball in the 2000 Summer Olympics.

I went out for a birthday dinner with Dana Antal, Kelly Bechard, and Tracy Luhowy, ex-teammates who are good friends. We had some wine and Italian food, not your typical athlete fare. No low-fat, no high-protein. It was high-fat, high-carb, great pasta, great wine. It was nice to catch up with old teammates. We talked about hockey, then not about hockey. It's interesting when your former teammates move on in their lives. Dana is pregnant. She and the other two have transitioned nicely into life after hockey. But when we started talking about the national team and the Olympics, everyone's passion for hockey was still there.

The book I'm reading, *The Metabolic Plan*, is about how to stay younger longer. Hockey is a youthful game. Being around it makes you feel youthful, and having a chance to go to the Olympics keeps you youthful. But there are still days when I am dead-dog tired and I fall into bed, exhausted, by 9 PM. Still, the fact that I made some personal bests in our fitness testing leading up to this camp shows I am doing the right things.

Our team fitness testing is tough. It takes about two days for a complete appraisal, and we do about ten different tests. In comparison, the National Hockey League Players' Association fitness testing policy allows about half a day for team testing, and they do about half the tests that we do!

We start with anthropometry, basically measuring body fat percentage. Our physiologists look for it to be in the 16 to 18 per cent range, although on our team it would go anywhere from 10 to 18 depending on the athlete and body type. We also perform what's called an incremental lactate test, which is done on a bike and basically tells us our aerobic capacity and provides us with training heart rates.

From there, we undergo strength tests such as bench press and chin-ups, plus vertical and horizontal jumps. They want us to perform a minimum of twelve full-hanging chin-ups and also be able to bench-press 1.1 to 1.2 times our body weight, four times. For me, this means bench pressing 190 to 200 pounds four times, which I can do.

We finish with the RHIET test, which essentially measures how fast we run forty metres and back, and what the drop-off rate in speed is when performing the exercise once every thirty seconds with six repetitions. The less drop-off time, the better the score. It is a hockey-specific test.

On day two we start with agility and speed tests, then move to the Wingate Test, which measures pure power over ten and thirty seconds. This may sound like a short test, but it's one of the hardest because it's an all-out effort. We always finish with the Léger-Boucher beep test, a running test requiring participants to run twenty metres forward and twenty metres back, prompted by a beep. As the test level increases, the beep gets faster and faster, until you can no longer keep up with the beep. It measures aerobic fitness and VO_2 max (the body's ability to use oxygen during exercise) and is always a fun way to finish when you are already fried from all the testing!

I went to bed pretty late after the birthday dinner, but I was up today at 6:30 AM for a 7:30 AM regeneration workout, which is basically a dynamic warm-up. In layman's terms, that means "moving stretching"—leg swings, running calf touches, a lot of track-based stuff that is more effective than just stretching statically. It preps the muscles for the next intensity. Generally, our warm-up starts with a dynamic warm-up then moves into some neural activation to get the brain and body going together. This includes sprint work and patters, which are light, quick steps that are seriously taxing but prep the neural system.

Our coaches are focused on ensuring that we maintain good habits, such as stopping in front of the net when taking a shot, not just skating away from it, which is so common in hockey. So in today's noon practice we did hard thirty-second one-on-one battling drills; working in the low zone; walking out of the corners; skills in small space. Dynamic things that we need to do more because we're a bit weak in those areas. We battled hard, seventy-five minutes of practice with only half the team, then the other half came out after us. I felt good despite being tired from last night. When my legs are heavy I need to go harder to get a good warm-up. I know it's going to take fifteen or twenty minutes and I know it's going to hurt. I need to blow the carbon out, like an old car! I'm thirty-one, now—Old, according to most of my teammates.

At the end of the session we decided to convey a message—that the practice was super hard—to the next group. We sent Brianne Jenner, the youngest rookie, into the dressing room. She's a quiet kid and doesn't like to swear. We told her to go in the room, throw her helmet, drop an F-bomb, and sit in her stall, and the rest of us would follow. And she did, she threw her helmet down, slammed her stick, and let loose an F-bomb. Caroline Ouellette tossed her gloves, and we all staggered in. The second group looked at us like we had three heads. What the hell is going on? What happened out there? We had them going for a few seconds, anyway. Then one of them figured it out, and there was a big laugh. Little jokes can help if there's tension or fatigue. They energize you, everyone has a laugh, and that brings you forward as a group. That's so valuable in a team sport.

EARLIER THIS WEEK I had a meeting with Peter Jensen, our sport psychologist. Peter has been to many Olympic Games and brings a wealth of knowledge to the table. I also enjoy and appreciate his laid-back demeanour. He has really seen it all in sport. We talked about playing with Certain Abandonment, which means playing recklessly enough, and freely enough, but being able to buy in and believe in the team system that you're playing. For example, if you're going to go for a pass and make a play, then you have to buy in with all your heart and soul. If you make it—great. If you don't, you live with the mistake you made but at least you bought in completely, not halfway in between.

That's my goal for the year, to play with that Certain Abandonment, to play free, just let things happen, be able to go out there and play the game I know how to play. It's always a challenge in an Olympic year. It can come down to one or two games that make the difference to an entire season.

After practice today we had a team meeting with Peter and talked about energy, what to do if we're under-energized or how to re-energize in certain game situations. My problem isn't usually being under-aroused or under-energized, it's usually the other way around. But there are definite strategies that I use, such as spending time with my son. He can take a lot of energy or give a lot of energy. I also rely on music, and I love reading inspirational books about people, or watching inspirational videos. Sometimes I go to the rink and feel like crap—I need energy, and I'm not in the game. It rarely happens but, sometimes it does. I talk to myself, using key words and phrases: "Jump. Fly. Roar. Gotta get up. Get in the warm-up. Go hard. Get that first shift. Get physical." I do whatever I have to do to get myself into it.

When you're over-aroused you need to know how to bring yourself down, such as using breathing techniques. I try to re-frame the situation: "Yeah, it's a gold medal game, but I've played in a hundred of these international games before. It's just another game on a big stage." Or I work to stay in the moment, knowing I'm going to make a first pass, get the puck in deep, have a really good first shift—not getting too far ahead of myself.

The less I think, the better off I am. I do all my thinking before I hit the rink. I like to go on autopilot, just let things happen. That's what I've been trying to do in practice, just focus on staying in the practice, enjoying it. And I know I'm actually "in" a practice when I pay attention to the drill as the coach draws it on the board. I like to go first in a drill, but sometimes when I'm zoned out I start the drill and mess it up. Then the girls call me the Drill Killer. There is nothing worse than being known as the team Drill Killer!

Our session with Peter lasted seventy-five minutes. We discussed how to turn things around if circumstances aren't going well. Some of this sport-psych stuff transfers well to the real world—things everybody can use every day, in business, with kids or family. As athletes, we learn to use these skills on a daily basis because we need them, especially when the stakes are high and we're in a gold medal situation, when twenty thousand people are expecting us to perform. We have to bring those habits into play every day. That's what this whole centralization is about—doing the important things every single day so that we can perform on the day it matters most.

I trained for a couple of summers with original Crazy Canuck skier Jungle Jim Hunter, and he often talked about "raising the bar." You have to raise the bar every day so that when you get to the Olympics, even if you think you need to raise the bar even more, you've already raised it and competed at that level every single day. So you can trust yourself when you get into competition. That's what it's about, trusting your preparation.

You can't just step into the Games and hope for the best. It doesn't work that way.

Wally Kozak, head scout and assistant coach to our team at the 2002 Winter Olympics, recently gave me an interesting article about having a stone in your shoe. You know how annoying that is—it gnaws at you, rubs you. So it's important to try to remove that stone from your shoe and be free. Sometimes you don't like how things are going, how the team is run or how a practice is done. But you have to remove the stone of your irritation and concentrate on what's important: moving toward the common goal.

I don't know if I'm there. Sometimes I am, sometimes not. Freeing myself from worrying about things just allows me to play, to go out and enjoy it, have fun with it. Some days, I can. On other days, stuff bugs the hell out of me.

I saw Wally at the rink today and he said, "Do you have any stones in your shoe?" I smiled at him and he said, "Ah, I think you do." We all do. We all have stones that we empty out here and there in different parts of our lives. That's the day-to-day grind of going through a process like this. I know every day is not going to be the best day. It's important to take it all in stride, and if I feel negative emotion, I need to release it as best as I can with whoever I can confide in, whoever I can trust, whoever can help me solve that problem.

Right now each day is kind of like Groundhog Day. They roll together with practices, training—there's not a lot of time for anything else. Even doing the dishes, managing to get food, it all has to be planned. It's a good thing I'm a planner.

AUGUST 15

Tonight we played our first game in this Olympic journey, a 7–2 win against Sweden. It also marked my two hundredth international game. I'm the only player on Team Canada to have played that many games so far. I actually didn't know it was my two hundredth game until a couple of days ago when our media guy, Chris Jurewicz, asked if I would do an interview with the *Calgary Herald* to set it up. It was a bit of a surprise. I guess it just means I've been around for a long time. It's hard to believe I've spent literally half my life on the national team. I was fifteen years old when I played my very first game in 1993. We played the U.S. in the Ottawa Civic Centre, and I scored my first goal. I remember it vividly, a slapshot from the top of circle.

How time flies—now it's two hundred international games later. If I was an NHL player, fifteen years of a career would probably add up to 1,200 to 1,500 games, but we don't play so many with the national women's team. We may play only ten to fifteen international games in a year, except in Olympic years, and the rest of the games are with our club or university teams.

In the dressing room prior to the game, the girls presented me with a cape, my Super Cape, which I proceeded to wear out on the pre-game skate. The girls got me to go out first. Then they waited, making me skate a lap in the cape all by myself, with Team Sweden on the ice. I looked like a fool, to the amusement of the coaching staff and many Hockey Canada officials and fans who were already in the building.

It was a special night. Hockey Canada presented me with a framed collage of different pictures of me throughout my career. My parents, Tom and Marilyn, joined me on the ice. Without my parents there is just no way I would have been able to get to this point. They were standing there with their Shooting Star hockey school jackets on—that was the hockey school that they ran and co-owned for fifteen years before stopping last year. The contribution they have given to the game of hockey, and to me and to my family, is beyond words.

Dad retired last year. He's been a teacher all his life, and now he can hang out at the rink. He's been coming to the practices every day. He's not very critical. He just observes but he likes to tell me who's looking good, which drills he likes. He doesn't offer much feedback. He never has, even when I was a kid. That was probably the greatest blessing, that my parents were so non-judgmental and non-critical, all the time. If we won or if we lost, it didn't really matter. It was more about whether I enjoyed it.

I think what my parents still care about most, even at this point in my career, is that I have fun playing the game. I know they sense at times that it's not so much fun. I think it bothers them, but they won't say anything. When I'm having fun, they're having fun. Dad just loves being at the rink. He loves dictating play-by-play through the game as it goes, which drives my mother crazy. But it's all very non-critical, which is wonderful because I'm critical enough myself.

Tomas and Noah also got back to town in time for the game, and it was so special to look up in the stands and see them there. Tomas was born in what is now the Czech Republic and came to Canada in 1994 to work as a skills coach with the Calgary Flames. He built his life in Canada around hockey. He has been not only my partner but also my coach. We've been together for ten years, and he's been my coach for five or six of those years. I've learned so much about hockey from him. He has given me so much, on and off the ice, and he has probably seen me play in at least half of those two hundred international games.

The game itself was disappointing. Winning 7–2 wasn't much of a challenge. Sweden has played five games to this point and they seemed tired, or disorganized. They seem to have regressed, maybe due to their young roster, or maybe they have haven't been playing at a high enough level. It was hard to stay in the game mentally. It was over after the first period, 3-0. But one exciting thing was that I played wing for the first time in a long time, with Meghan Agosta at centre and Marie-Philip Poulin on the left side. Each of us had two or three great scoring opportunities, and we didn't score. I missed a flat-out breakaway. Brutal! I whiffed on the puck.

I felt really good physically. It seems I have a lot of speed. I was making plays out there, and playing on the wing is different; it gives me a chance to get the puck more, and I don't have to come deep into the defensive zone and play like a third defenceman. I can hang out and conserve my energy, which is beneficial. But it goes against the nature of who I am—intense, all out, go get the puck, get into the battles. Perhaps it will be good to mix it up and give teams another look as they won't know how to defend me on the wing.

WE HAVE A BIG WEEK coming up—three games against the under-22 squad (I'll play in two of them), plus practices. In two weeks we are off to the Hockey Canada Cup in Vancouver. My head is spinning. There are charity events looming, some kids are coming to the rink tomorrow, stuff needs to be signed. A lot of people want a lot of things. I just have to find a way to say no sometimes without upsetting people.

Being an athlete is a lifestyle. It's not just about stepping on the ice. It's a job, everything goes into it. In a way it's an extremely selfish existence. You're concerned about what you eat, how you sleep, how you feel. Sometimes this lifestyle is hard on the family. I missed Tomas and Noah dearly when they were in Vernon, but at the same time I had a chance to focus on what I needed to do. I get a lot of business work done when I'm on my own. For example, I receive two or three charitable or item requests per week—almost per day, it seems now. Saying no is one thing I've had to learn to do over the course of my career. Right now I'm saying no a lot because I want to keep my schedule open. I want to just focus on being a hockey player and doing my job every day on the ice. The more I can manage that, the better.

AUGUST 21

We've played three games now, the first against Sweden and two against the under-22 team, who we beat 4–3 then 5–2. Unfortunately, we lost young player Jennifer Wakefield in the process. She separated her shoulder and will be out for a couple of weeks.

I have trouble falling asleep after a game because I just live it over and over in my mind for hours. So it's been short turnarounds to our morning workouts at nine o'clock. Some days I try to come home after the workout, nap, then go for lunch at Fuel for Gold and have Chef Aurelio's wonderful meals, which are designed for Olympic athletes. For $5.25 you can get a thirty-dollar gourmet meal, balanced nutritionally.

We also had an Olympic meeting this week, talking about tickets, accommodation, and family and friends being at the Games, and we watched a video about the Olympic preparation in Vancouver. It gave me goosebumps. I got that "Olympic feeling." It's hard to explain the "Olympic feeling." It's a certain excitement and energy that comes over me. It's such positive energy. It's very uplifting, almost like an out-of-this-world experience that arises but once every four years. And it's something very few people ever get to experience.

We were shown the athletes' village and what our accommodation will look like. We'll be on Floor 11, the men's team on Floor 7. It gives us confidence to know our facilities are probably the best they've ever been for a Canadian team at the Olympics. Also, our families and friends are going to be taken care of through three different programs: the Petro-Canada program, Homestay Program, and the Ladies First Hockey Foundation, which has raised money over the last five or six years to help our families go to the Games. Led by Tim Harrison and supported by the *Globe and Mail* and key sponsors, it raises money directly for the players on the team. To this point it's raised $130,000. It has helped us so much.

The energy in the room was electric and genuine. It was the perfect timing for such a presentation. It reminded everybody about what we're striving for and what an opportunity it is for us.

THE DAYS ARE LONG, they always are at this time of year when the coaches are trying to pack everything in. It will be nice to move on to the Hockey Canada Cup in Vancouver in a couple of weeks. The men's team is coming in next week. It's an exciting atmosphere. Every day is a chance to get better, a chance to experience something new in this Olympic journey, even if I've been there before.

Sometimes I try to get out of my comfort zone, do things that I don't normally do every day, whether it's cool down right away, change, and leave, not hang around the rink as much as usual. Maybe it means getting out on the ice early, trying different things. When I step on the ice I'm in my element, that's where I feel most comfortable. No matter how bad the day goes, something good can always come from being on the ice, doing what I love to do, living the dream.

One day this week I went for sushi with Syl after practice. When we get together we just exchange stories and have a lot of laughs. In a team sport you're around the same people all the time, and it's important to get out of that element and hang around with different people, key people who can really help you in life. For example, I talked with Wally Kozak at the rink this week—he's like a father figure to me. We talked hockey—the old Russian system, the new systems, players coming up, perspectives on the game. He is a hockey genius. After talking to him, I always step away feeling good about everything and myself. In these situations I need to surround myself with people like Wally and Syl.

Today was a marathon day. I had to be at the rink for 9 AM practice. At 12:30 PM I had an interview with CTV about Right to Play, an organization that utilizes sport to improve the lives of disadvantaged children throughout the world. In between, I dropped the puck for a kids' game that was part of a hockey school program. Somewhere in the middle of all that, I watched a little of the under-18s–versus–under-22s game.

I also had a meeting with team dietitian Kelly Anne Carter-Erdman. For three days we were asked to document everything we ate. She took the info and came up with a personal profile, which basically tells each of us if we're eating well and what we need to get more of, or less. The first of my three days showed I consumed 3,500 calories. The next was an 1,100-calorie day, where I think I ate twice because we were so busy and I didn't have any snacks. The other day was more my norm, about 2,800 calories. I'm all over the place. I have to increase my protein a little more and really watch the post-game recovery meal to make sure I'm getting enough of the appropriate proteins, carbs, and fats.

It's a complex thing, but the nutrition aspect of being an athlete is extremely important. It's fuel for your body. I don't care what kind of VO$_2$ max you have, or how fit you are. You're not going anywhere if you don't have the proper fuel in your body. It's important, especially this year with so many games and so much travel. If a feeling of hunger comes over you, it's almost too late. You have to keep fuelled by eating throughout the day.

At 2:30 PM, half our forward group had a workout with James Gattinger at the Volleydome. He's a strength and conditioning coach who has worked with the men's Olympic team and the Calgary Flames. I've worked with him, on and off, since I was fifteen years old. He's been around hockey for a long time and he understands the importance of having a bit of fun. We played volleyball. It's pretty funny to watch hockey players play other sports. Sometimes we're not the most graceful people out there, but we get the job done and we certainly compete hard against each other. Nobody wanted the game to stop. Afterward we lifted weights for thirty minutes, then I headed up to Kelsey's for an hour and a half of resistance stretching and strengthening through a range of motion.

There are many times during a game where you're hit or pushed off balance or stretched beyond your max, circumstances that can result in injury. These exercises stretch you throughout your range of motion and strengthen you to ensure you have strength at the end range, which is where we are usually weak. I value this work as much as a good massage. I heard about it through Andy, who works closely with American swimmer Dara Torres. At age forty-one, she won three silver medals at the 2008 Summer Olympics in Beijing. We went to Florida in the off-season this year to meet her two gurus of resistance stretching, and they taught Kelsey the program. They also worked with me intensively. I've been doing it weekly, and it's a key to my success, or any success that I'm going to have.

THAT WAS MY DAY. I came home and grabbed some of Aurelio's well-balanced Fuel for Gold meals that he made for me last night—some chicken and vegetables and rice pilaf. I cleaned my house, something I haven't done for three or four days. I just let everything go because it's been so crazy this week. I've gone through centralization three or four times now, and I can't remember the first few weeks being this jam-packed with meetings and so many activities.

There are dishes all over the place. I don't like it when my house is in disarray. I like to have things neat and organized. When the house is clean, my mind is clean. I need to keep things simple, routine, uncluttered. That creates more chances to rest and focus, as inspirational speaker Lou Holtz would say, on the W-I-N. What's Important Now.

I need to decompress and rest before we really get into our season. Noah heads back to school next week. These are exhausting days, long days: having 9 AM practice after a late game, being on the ice for two hours in the morning and another hour in the afternoon workout. But we're getting through it. The girls are being troopers and doing the right things. So far, so good. I like what I see and I like the way we're coming together.

AUGUST 24

I had a good day off yesterday. I spent it with Noah. He had been in Windsor for a week with my sister, Jane, and they had a great time, although I missed him terribly. Life has been so busy, I wouldn't have seen him much the last few days even if he had been here. I think he had more fun with Jane than with Boring Old Mom, as he likes to call me! Kids grow so fast. He brings me a lot of joy and a lot of perspective. He's a positive distraction.

Today was the start of the men's camp. The official gong show begins. The media is speculating about who will play with whom, who will be the captain, who will be the starting goalie, who will represent Canada at the Olympics in February.

We got to the rink for 9 o'clock and had a 10 o'clock practice. The Gatorade Institute was in to perform their sweat testing. It totally cracked us up because we had to produce a urine sample, get weighed, and go on the ice for a one-hour practice that was supposed to be a flow sweat practice. It turned into a bit of a bag skate—a series of intense drills that seriously tire you out, usually meted out by the coach as a form of punishment. Well, our coach wasn't too happy with our effort after the first twenty minutes. She dropped a few profanities, called us out, and threw in a battle drill. We had been laughing and joking after the first fifteen minutes, nobody was really sweating. Five minutes into the battle drill we were all bent over, dying on the ice.

After an hour they took off our sweat pads and checked for lost fluids. Some of the girls lost two to three pounds. I didn't lose anything—I stayed the same weight. That's good. It tells them I'm probably drinking enough fluid and staying hydrated. Also, I tend not to sweat that much.

Overall it was a good practice. My lungs were exploding, it was pretty intense. I cooled down then went home. I was able to lie down for about thirty minutes, put my legs up, close my eyes, and rest, try to re-energize. Sometimes all I need is twenty to thirty minutes of peaceful rest. Mom had taken Noah and his buddy Isaac to a corn maze. Mom has been so helpful and supportive, especially at times when Tomas and I are busy or on the road. When things get crazy she is there to help with Noah, the Little Monster, and I'm so grateful.

Later in the day I took my Dad to the men's practices. We sat there with Andy and watched the guys skate. Two groups came out on the ice. The first, we determined, was maybe the B squad and the second the A squad, which included Sidney Crosby and Jarome Iginla.

It was funny to watch the first group come out. They were a little rusty. But the second group, some of the guys looked really good. I was impressed with Crosby, Iginla, Duncan Keith, Jay Bouwmeester, Rick Nash—they all looked very good. So did Martin St. Louis, who is explosive and dynamic. It's amazing to watch these guys, real pros: Scott Niedermayer, the way he skates; Chris Pronger, his physical size and ability; Robyn Regehr, how solid he is. It's going to be interesting to see who is eventually chosen for the Olympic team.

Everybody and their dog is in town, from equipment sponsors to the media. They all want a piece of these guys. I certainly feel for Sidney and guys like him who are in high demand all the time. They handle it pretty well considering what they have to go through on a daily basis. There's also the continuing Dany Heatley saga, with him asking to be traded from the Senators at the end of last season then refusing to waive his no-trade clause when Ottawa made a deal with Edmonton.

I feel for him. He's had a difficult go in the media. Maybe he didn't handle it well, his agents didn't, whoever is giving him advice. But we're all human, we all want to do well and not make bad decisions. I think he has, unfortunately, made a few in his career. He's a great player and he is certainly a talent on the ice. It will be interesting to see what he does in the first half of the season, to see if he can lock his spot.

But there are also going to be some sleepers. Patrick Sharp might be one. We'll also see how Shea Weber does, he's a talented young kid.

Dad and I both love the game and sitting and talking with people at the rink. This week has an Olympic feel with the spotlight and media circus around it. I laugh because we get the trickle-down effect on the women's team. These media people, you don't see a lot of them for years, but when the Olympics are looming they suddenly show up at the rink and pretend they're interested when they probably don't care three out of the four years. Ah well, that's the nature of what we do. Be grateful for what we have—that's how we have to look at it.

I picked up Noah, and we went home. We made a gluten-free pizza and we talked about his school as we ate. I think he's nervous about Grade 4, but I know he's going to do great. He's a pretty mature, worldly kid, and he's a sensitive little guy, too. I know it's hard on him when I'm gone all day. I might only see him for a couple of hours every day right now because that's our schedule.

Some day, I hope he looks back and thinks, "What my Mom did was pretty cool, I'm proud of her." He might not understand that now. The other day he told me he *loves* me, but he's not sure he *likes* me because I'm gone a lot! That's difficult for me to hear, and it weighs on me. I feel guilty. As females, maybe that happens to us more—that societal pressure on mothers. It can be tough, and separation is really hard. Noah often asks me when I'm going to retire so I can hang out more. He also tells me I'm obsessed with hockey. He knows the commitment that goes into it.

I asked him if he wanted to come to the men's practice. He could hang out at the rink and watch Sidney Crosby. He said, "Why would I do that, Mom? It's so boring. I'm going to stay home and play Wii."

He's pretty grounded. He's a beautiful boy, and I'm very proud of him and everything he's accomplished in his short little life. Every day he teaches me about perspective and what's important, because at the end of the day he couldn't care less about winning, losing, scoring, not scoring.

AUGUST 26

We practised at the Saddledome today. It was my first taste of seeing what the Olympic atmosphere will be like. There was more media there today than for a Stanley Cup final. Okay, they weren't there to watch us, or the sledge team. But Hockey Canada did a nice job of including the sledge and women's teams in the day's schedule. The sledge team practised first, then the women's team, and then the men's team split into two groups. By the time we were starting our practice, the media was filing into the building and actually watching us.

The ice was terrible, but the girls were really keyed up. It was exciting. It's not very often we get to be in that type of atmosphere. I've been in this situation many times over the years, with the national team and in my time playing professional hockey, so it doesn't get to me or distract me anymore. Some of our younger players, their eyes were wide open. There was a lot of energy, and sometimes it's helpful to have that energy injected into a practice environment.

For me, being in the Saddledome is always special. I watched my first Olympics in person in Calgary in 1988. I was a ten-year-old kid and I was inspired. Every time I step in the Saddledome I think about the '88 Olympics and what that did for me as a kid, and what the Olympics will do for so many young kids in 2010.

The practice was high tempo, lots of flow, lots of run-and-gun. Then we had to wait for an hour to get our pictures taken with the men's team and the sledge team. During that time I did a scrum. Doing the media stuff, this is sometimes the annoying part of the job. I held court with probably ten to fifteen reporters, and many of these people I would never see until it's an Olympic year. Then they come out of the woodwork.

We all knew they were there to watch the men's team, that probably seven of ten wouldn't be there if the men weren't there. But they were in the building covering the men's team so maybe they'd been told to do some stories on the women's team, too. Or they'd been told to ask what the women think of the men being there. I know that's part of the job, and I'm very happy to educate them. That's what it turned out to be, an education session. It was kind of hilarious.

Donna Spencer, who is a beat writer for the Canadian Press, covers our team relentlessly and is a dedicated, knowledgeable writer. She asked a lot of the questions, and everybody else just stood around and took the sound bites. But some of the guys asked questions like: "Do you think the men are upstaging you? What do you think about the men being here?" My answer was simple: "That's their reality, they're in a million-dollar business, they're driving a lot of revenue for the game, the profile, the media, the expectations. Our reality is a bit different, and we're just happy to be included."

That's really the way I feel. Geez, I wish I made ten million dollars a season. I wish I could play an eighty-two-game schedule and fly on private jets and play in twenty-thousand-seat arenas. But our game is growing. One day I hope we'll get there. But I don't feel slighted in any way. Probably part of that is because when you're in Hockey Canada you really aren't treated that much differently. You know the men get a few things here and there that the women don't get but everybody accepts that. We feel like we've come a long way.

In this situation I run into guys like Shane Doan, Jarome Iginla, Ryan Smyth, Sidney Crosby, and there is mutual respect. They appreciate the fact that we put our careers and lifestyles on the line to play for very little money, for the love of the game. We can share experiences. As I said to the media, "We've had many women who have been to more Olympic Games than some of these guys." The Games are a different atmosphere. It is not a Stanley Cup final. You're one sport within many when you get to the Games—just a little fish in the big sea. It's a different dynamic, and there are things we can offer. The men ask us questions.

And watching the sledge team! These guys are strapped into a sled and they propel themselves up and down the ice using picks on the bottom of sticks. They have amazing upper body strength. They shoot a puck—using one arm—eighty miles an hour. That's harder than most of our players can shoot. They're regular people just like we are. They have jobs and still find a way to play for the love of the game. There's a real mutual respect between everyone. I give Hockey Canada a lot of credit for bringing us all together.

BUT OUR SCHEDULE has been totally rearranged thanks to the men's team being in town. It's been crazy. For the last two days I've left my place at seven in the morning and returned home at eleven or twelve o'clock at night. It's not the on- or off-ice training that's exhausting, it's having to do the meet-and-greets.

We went to a corporate dinner tonight. The Hockey Canada Foundation hosted the men's team, the women's team, and the sledge team, so we mixed and mingled with corporate Calgary. Many people who supported it paid $1,500 to sit at the table and have a chance to be around the Olympic teams. Gen. Rick Hillier, former Chief of the Defence Staff of the Canadian Forces, gave a speech relating hockey to the military in terms of leadership and going into battle. He brought in some soldiers, introduced them and talked about their stories in Afghanistan and why they are heroes. Such a dynamic presentation!

Pierre McGuire, the event host, also went around the room and interviewed a few of the players, myself included. He asked me what the difference was between losing the final in a shootout at the 2005 worlds and winning Olympic gold in 2006. I said the difference is always about bringing your best on the day when it matters the most and playing great hockey. When we go into 2010 the focus can't be about winning the gold medal. The focus has to be on playing the game, enjoying the game, and putting our best hockey together.

Everybody is talking about going for three gold medals in Vancouver: men's and women's gold at the Olympics and gold in sledge hockey at the Paralympics. Triple gold—pressure and expectation! That's all everyone talks about at these corporate dinners. Sometimes we need to deflect that pressure and expectation away from ourselves. Don't get me wrong, I like those dinners and the environment. It's very exciting. But at times I prefer to be away from it and be focused on keeping my little joy bubble around me.

Sometimes it's hard. These events are demanding in a different way. You're out late. All the temptations are there. You can have a few glasses of wine, go out, mix and mingle. But you still have to get up the next morning and perform at practice, and that's the most important thing. So I'm trying to shut it down early these nights.

AUGUST 27

Forty-six guys, representing the best in Canadian hockey, got together tonight for a shinny game with no hitting, part of a four-day camp that really isn't determining anything for sure about who will make the Olympic team. What happened? About twenty thousand people filled the Saddledome. Only in Canada!

People in red and white. Crazy fans. Kids glued to the action. Roberto Luongo plays for the Vancouver Canucks, fierce divisional rivals of the Calgary Flames. But the fans were cheering "Lou! Lou!" At first I thought it was "Boo! Boo!" but it was "Lou!" The appreciation they had for Luongo, wearing a Canadian team logo, was incredible. People got into the Canadiana of the night—it wasn't the NHL anymore. It was about the Olympics. We're trying to win a gold medal. It was really special. The fans were serious, and so were the players.

I talked to Sidney Crosby a couple of days ago and asked, "What do you think about all this?" He said, "Hey, we're not going out for beer after these events, we're going to bed and we're getting ready, we want to impress." Shane Doan, same thing: "There are a lot of good players here, the tempo's really high, it's pretty for real."

You could see it. Ryan Smyth played a helluva game for a guy who everyone says is a grinder/checker/fringe player. He must have a heart of gold. He scored, he set up plays, made things happen. He won't go down lightly. Duncan Keith, he's a young kid, he's a dark horse. But he's got to be there. He skates too well not to be there. Shea Weber, playing on smaller ice, is a big, strong guy. Niedermayer is thirty-six years old and he can still go with the puck.

It was so special to be in that building and be a part of it. Our whole team was there. In fact, Mike Babcock, the men's Olympic team coach, had come up to me on Wednesday and said he admired my career, he had a thirteen-year-old daughter and could

I sign something for her. He said he'd like to talk to our team so we arranged for him to come into the room and say a few words after the first period. He talked about playing under pressure and how we're here for a reason. He talked about the times players are thinking one thing and the coaching staff is thinking another, how we've got to ask questions. He also talked about being mentally tough.

It was great for our team to see an NHL coach who is so intense, so driven, so detail-oriented, so prepared. It was interesting that so much of what he said, and his methods and mannerisms, are traits and approaches we see in our head coach, Mel Davidson. It's amazing how similar they are.

It's no coincidence Mike Babcock is the coach of a Stanley Cup champion team. His intensity is reflected in the players on the ice. They didn't want to disappoint. It's good for our girls to be in that environment and to see, in many ways, these guys are no different from us. They warm up and cool down the same way we do. They wear the same clothes, they have the same kinds of sticks.

The Olympics may still be months away, but the outpouring and interest in the Red and White scrimmage here just shows the level of Olympic anticipation and expectation brewing in the Canadian public. I can only imagine the intensity of the atmosphere that will unfold in Vancouver.

Perhaps the only person unimpressed by the proceedings was Noah. At the end of the night he said to me, "Mom, I sure hope that all this pays off."

And I said, "Pays off for what?"

And he said, "Well, down the road, I just really hope it pays off, because I've had to go to a lot of games over the years."

I just cracked up. It's hilarious because his parents are so involved in the game. Yet the last thing he ever wants to do is be in a hockey rink. He has access to the best of everything in hockey, to meet the best players and have a great experience in the game. But he just has no interest in it.

AUGUST 30

It is Sunday and we're in Vancouver for the pre-Olympic tournament, the Hockey Canada Cup. Basically it's a four-nation tournament featuring Canada, the United States, Sweden, and Finland, all of whom are gearing up for the Olympics. All our tournament games will be played in GM Place, making this an Olympic test event (though we aren't playing any of these games at the UBC rink where some of our Olympic games will take place). Although the tournament doesn't mean anything, we want to have a good showing and set the standard. Victory would set us up well in terms of confidence, which is what we need coming off a 4–1 loss to the United States in the World Championships last spring.

THERE IS A LOT of hockey yet to be played before the 2010 Olympics, but it's no surprise people want to talk about Canada versus the United States. It's a rivalry that has existed since the first world women's hockey championship was held in Ottawa in 1990, where Canada defeated the U.S. 5–2 in the final. The two teams also met in the finals of the 1992, '94, and '97 world tournaments, and each time Canada emerged as champion.

Women's hockey debuted as an Olympic sport at the 1998 Winter Games in Nagano. There was a lot of pressure and expectation for Canada to win that inaugural women's gold medal, but the Americans beat us 7–4 in the round robin tournament and defeated us 3–1 in the final to take the gold.

The next four World Championships—1999, 2000, 2001, and 2004—went to Canada, as did the 2002 Olympic gold medal, which we won by defeating the Americans 3–2 in the final. That was an especially satisfying victory because the U.S. had won all our pre-Olympic series games leading up to Salt Lake City, and they were also favoured as the home country.

Our world winning streak ended in Sweden in 2005, when the Americans won the ninth women's world hockey championship by beating us 1–0 in a shootout. But a year later they were playing "O Canada" after the Olympic final in Torino. We won that gold medal by defeating Sweden 4–1. The Swedes upset the Americans in the semifinals, and the U.S. had to settle for bronze. In 2007 we defeated the U.S. 5–1 to give Canada a ninth world championship.

Since then the Americans have been number one, winning the world title in 2008 after edging us 4–3, and last year taking the world championship again by defeating us 4–1. We were a fragile team after that loss. We lacked confidence, identity, goals, and direction, and we questioned our leadership. Through that whole process we held players' meetings where we decided we had to be more accountable. To her credit, Mel took some of the feedback we offered as players and committed to being more open and approachable.

She put together her Olympic staff, and as a group they came back to us with a very strong message: "This is the way it's going to be. If you don't like it, leave." That's what our team needed to hear. By the time we hit our boot camp in Dawson Creek we were ready to work, ready to do whatever it took because we were tired of losing.

WHEN WE ARRIVED HERE in Vancouver this week it was 30 degrees—it hardly felt like hockey season. I lived here in 2000 when I played softball for Simon Fraser University. I love the city. There's so much to do, it has a real west coast feel, a laid-back feel. It is the biggest city to ever play host to the Winter Olympics, and I think they're going to do a great job. On a nice day it's the most incredible city in the world.

After we arrived we walked to GM Place from the Sheraton hotel, a twenty-minute walk in beautiful weather, in our flip-flops and shorts. We casually wheeled into the arena with no security and no accreditation check, just a few people here and there around the rink. We came off the ice after practice, and there were three or four media cameras, that was it. Come Games time there will be people everywhere, security everywhere, checks everywhere, media everywhere, attention everywhere.

Out on the ice, I imagined scoring the winning goal, hearing the crowd and feeling the atmosphere in the building. It flashed through my mind: thirty seconds left, come down, take the puck, slapshot, score, then a mob scene and celebration. It felt very good, very Olympic, and I'm very excited to be in that Olympic atmosphere and to skate in the building.

The ice is different, it's smaller than the Father David Bauer arena, where we train, so that will be an adjustment for us. We'll see how the team reacts this week to playing on that smaller surface. The ice feels different, hard but chippy. The pucks were bouncing around quite a bit.

Our dressing room today was the same room we had in 2002 when we played our last pre-Olympic game against the U.S. I remember it vividly because we lost 2-1, and after the game I flipped out because I was sick of losing. I really lost it. I threw my equipment across the room, started yelling. It was just the raw emotion of losing seven in a row to the Americans.

When we walked into the dressing room today, Colleen Sostorics and I had a little chuckle about it. I remembered where I was sitting, she remembered where I was sitting. She had tried to stop me, to tell me to calm down, as I stormed out of the room to talk to the media. But I think that's where we turned it around, coming out of that Vancouver game. In 2002, going to the Olympics in Salt Lake, we had to get real as a team and figure out where we needed to get better. It happened in Vancouver, and we went on to win that gold medal. So I have a lot of memories from this arena.

WE DID A MEET-AND-GREET with the VANOC people last night. There are a lot of extra demands on our time with the Olympics in Canada, a challenge for us because we need to balance those demands with ensuring we get enough rest. I'm looking forward to this week. It's going to be a good test. It's important for us to send a message and come out of here with a victory. The coaches laid down a challenge for everyone to play consistent or they might not be in that final game at the end of the week. Everybody's on edge because it's still a tryout process. There will be cuts at some point. It's hard to perform when somebody's always looking down on you, critiquing your performance. But we're all in the same situation. For some it's more difficult than for others.

We probably know who the top six or nine forwards are going to be and who is fighting for the last three spots. If we wrote them down everybody would probably write the same names. But everybody still has to perform. The most important thing is the individual performance has to be there for the team performance to be there.

It's going to be interesting to get the feel of this Olympic city. Will there be fans in the stands for this tournament? My guess is it will probably be fairly empty until the finals. It would be great to have it full but I've heard there hasn't been a lot of talk about the event in the media here. Maybe as the weekend comes closer, when we play the U.S., people will come out to see what is potentially the Olympic final matchup.

Tomorrow we have our first game, against Sweden. This is where we really start moving forward, testing ourselves, pursuing that Olympic gold.

SEPTEMBER 22

There are times when it's better not to say anything at all. That's how I've felt the past couple of weeks since the end of the Hockey Canada Cup. The final was another game against the U.S. The result was a scenario that is all too familiar.

We outplayed them, marginally. We outshot them. We out-chanced them. But we didn't win. We lost 2-1. It sucked.

I sat in the dressing room afterward and just shook my head in disbelief. We still can't buy a win against them. Our team pressed a lot, but we didn't shoot the puck well. We had too many of our shots blocked. We played with energy, we played hard and did all the little things, but they got two lucky bounces. Penalties probably cost us as well. It was disappointing.

It was a weird atmosphere. The crowd was definitely into it, the fans at GM Place were just waiting for us to break it open and they would have exploded. We never gave them that opportunity.

What can I say about a tournament that comes at the very start of what is going to be a long Olympic process? It was supposed to be a test event, not just for us but for the Olympic organizers as they work through things in preparing for the Games in February. The tournament started interestingly enough, with Finland edging the U.S. 3-2 in the first game on the first day, while we followed with a 7-0 shutout of Sweden. Three days later, the U.S. beat us 4-2. In the final we managed a single goal, and you're not going to win too many games off just one goal.

Losing in the building where the Olympics are going to be, how bad is that? If you win you say that's a great opportunity, to feel what it's like to win. But standing at the blue line, waiting for the post-game ceremonies, was driving me crazy. I couldn't wait to get the hell off the ice. We had to stand there and watch the Americans take their gold medal. I don't want to feel like that six months from now. We lost. I thought, "Look at them, they are going to get a little bit cocky." And I tried to find ways to convince myself it doesn't really matter.

Ultimately it doesn't matter because between now and February we are going to be in a totally different place as a team. I can see it. I can feel it. We will grow, particularly as our young players develop, as we find our feet beneath us, so to speak. It's just about patience. It's also about leaving nothing unsaid.

We returned to Calgary. We had work to do.

THE DAYS AFTER THE Hockey Canada Cup were tough for our team. In times like these you have to talk to people who can help you. Someone I rely on, someone I go to for advice as a friend, is Bobby Clarke, former GM of the Philadelphia Flyers and a great player himself. I met him in 1998 in Nagano, where he was GM of the men's team. He invited me to the Flyers camps in 1998 and '99. From there we have maintained a good friendship. We talk once in a while, and I like to watch the Flyers games. We try to connect once or twice a year. There's a general respect that he has for me as an athlete and for the women's game, and he played at a time when it wasn't cool for women to play hockey. I respect who he was as a player and who he is as a person. He's tough as nails and doesn't make excuses. He had a finger that had been bugging him for a long time. What did he do? He had it amputated!

We talked a lot about the game, about the fact that if you don't have emotion in the dressing room or if you don't have good leadership, no matter how good a group you have, it's very difficult to win. We talked about how Xs and Os are the easiest things to teach, but what's harder is to draw the best out of the players; also how, as players, you always know first what's going on inside a team before the coaching staff or anyone else outside the team. We also talked about the importance of trusting your gut. It's my responsibility, as team captain, to be the voice of the players and to be able to express things, whether or not it's comfortable or easy for me—and sometimes it isn't. He's a good sounding board, willing to help and to give me advice.

I also talked to Mark Messier recently. I spoke with him about our leadership and where we're going. He was my hockey idol when I was growing up. He knows I'm a big fan of his, maybe even a super fan, but in this case I was just looking for a professional opinion, getting advice from someone who's been there and done it in many different situations. He was helpful and offered some great advice related to the spiritual, physical, and emotional aspects of hockey.

On the weekend I was able to work with Andy and with Mark Lindsay, a well-known chiropractor and ART soft-tissue specialist. He came up to Calgary from working with the Denver Broncos—his resume also includes Tiger Woods and the New York Yankees—and he spent two hours with me, adjusting my body. He did some deep soft-tissue work to relieve some of the false sciatica I tend to get down the right side of my leg when my glute or hip muscles get too tight. He's married to Kate Pace Lindsay, a former Canadian Olympic skier and a world downhill champion. It's important to have those types of people around you because they operate on a different energy vibration than most people. They tend to have a joy and a passion for what they do, and a drive to want to be the best.

Meanwhile, in two days we start our sixty-game schedule with four games—Thursday, Friday, Saturday, Sunday—against Midget AAA boys' teams.

OCTOBER 1

Sometimes when I am working Noah likes to hang around with me and play Lego. I often ask him what he thinks about life, his Mom playing hockey. More often than not his answer is: "I think it's boring!"

Lately we've been talking about the Olympics. This is what Noah Alexander Pacina, born April 5, 2000, Mr. Legomaniac, Pianoman, Soccer Specialist, Swimming Guru, and Hip Hop Artist du Jour, had to say:

"Noah, what do you think about this whole Olympic thing?"

"I think hockey's weird," he said.

"Why is hockey weird?"

"'Cos it's kind of boring."

"What did you do in the gold medal game of the Hockey Canada Cup a while ago? Were you reading something?

"Yeah, I was reading a book."

"So, the game went on, 8,500 people were going crazy, and you were..."

"...very quietly reading my book."

"Do you think in the Olympic Games, if your Mom is playing in the gold medal final, you might actually be sitting there reading a book?"

"Maybe. Probably a 99-thousand-point-nine per cent chance that I might be doing that."

"Remember the other night? We were watching a program on TV about the top ten Olympic moments, and at number two was your mom's team from the Salt Lake City Games. Remember the question you asked when we were sitting there? You asked: 'How do you...'"

"... get to the Olympics?"

"And I said, 'Well, look at your mother.' And you said, 'That's boring, that's boring to do what you have to do to get to the Olympics, Mom.' So, all in all, what do you think the Olympics are all about?"

"Just trying to win medals and trying to work really hard and trying to get a gigantic gold medal, or whatever."

"What do you think the Olympics mean to the world?"

"A big thing. It's kind of special."

"Why is it kind of special?"

"I'm not sure if men are in the Olympics, too, but I think it's just girls. I'm not exactly sure."

"No, there're men there, there are lots of sports."

"Oh yeah, there's skiing, too."

"If you were going to go to the Olympics, what sport would you compete in?"

"Ummmm, do they have such a thing as football in the Olympics?"

"Ah, no."

"Argggh. Well, then it would either be basketball or something else."

"What about swimming, or skiing—two sports that you do?"

"I'm not sure, some chance though."

"But ultimately that's not what you're interested in. What are you interested in?"

"Lego."

"Thank you, Noah Alexander Pacina. Best wishes in building the spaceship Lego you're building right now. It looks very cool!"

Noah has probably two hundred Lego models that he has built in our basement. He's very creative with his hands. It's great for me that he has so many diverse interests because I don't have to be in another hockey rink. I'm in a hip hop studio; at the swimming pool; in the basement hanging out and playing; taking him to piano lessons; or we're out riding our bikes. Noah keeps it real, especially when I'm at the rink thinking something is the end of the world.

PREPARING FOR AN OLYMPIC GAMES is a long and arduous process. It's important to have a little fun along the way. Recently Mel and I had a discussion, and I said, "We've been together for 106 days, something like that, and we've never actually had a fun team activity, for a whole day, without there being a practice or a training workout. It would be great if we could go golfing."

So I arranged to have the girls and the staff—thirty-two people, eight foursomes—play at Elbow Springs Golf Club. We had a little scramble, and it was a lot of fun, it turned out to be a beautiful day. We tried to pair up golfers with non-golfers, and girls who typically wouldn't hang out with each other. It was a fun day, nice to spend time in a non-hockey environment. These activities help players get to know one another in a non-threatening atmosphere, away from the daily routine.

We came to the rink today, and everybody was refreshed and happy. We had a great practice, a lot of tempo and a lot of skating. Last week our team leadership group also had a meeting—the group consists of Jennifer Botterill, Jayna Hefford, Caroline Ouellette, myself, Kim St-Pierre, Gillian Ferrari, and Becky Kellar. We discussed where the team was at, what was working, what wasn't. Then the captains—Ouellette, Hefford, and myself—met with Mel and talked about specific things that we'd like to see: more positive feedback, a more positive atmosphere, and more energy around our team. Mel took it well. She was very professional. She agreed the coaching staff should be more engaged, she agreed they should get into things, have fun. She also challenged us, suggesting people also take responsibility for their own confidence and a positive team atmosphere. It was a very good discussion. It's been a tough time for our team lately, not being able to generate wins against the U.S. Keeping communication open between players and coaches is key.

The atmosphere has been fantastic since we had that talk. We've responded with some good practices. Doug Lidster and Peter Smith, the assistant coaches, have stepped up with some good drills and tempo. Peter Smith is the head coach at McGill, and he's had a lot of success. He demands a lot from his players but he also manages to keep things light.

We're moving the puck really well, as a group and moving ahead. We've had some wins against the Midget AAA teams, and we're preparing to travel to Victoria for a game against the United States, our first of six pre-Olympic exhibition games. I can't wait to play them again. Victoria is a key game for us.

OCTOBER 4

Playing on a national or Olympic hockey team is more than just scoring goals or winning games. Elite athletes have the potential to be great role models for young people, something I have tried to keep in mind throughout my career. The potential to impact someone's life became evident when we arrived here in Victoria and attended the PacificSport Celebration of Women in Sport event. About a thousand people were in attendance at the convention centre, including a lot of young girls and athletes from the community, with our team as special guests.

I sat next to Doug Lidster. He won a Stanley Cup with the Rangers and played with the great players of his day. He was a good defenceman himself. One of the best things about having a guy like Doug with the team is his knowledge of the game. He knows important subtleties that only an athlete, playing at the calibre he played at, would know about, such as where to put your stick on a one-on-one, how to block in front of the net.

Throughout the night young girls came up and asked us for autographs. At one point Doug said to me, "Who did you admire growing up, Wick? You must have had role models."

I said, "I didn't have any role models, or female hockey players to look up to. I didn't know who they were, they just didn't have the exposure, the visibility. I admired the players you played with—Messier, Gretzky—the closest I came to meeting Mark Messier was seeing him in a towel at Northlands Coliseum. I never had the courage to ask him for his autograph."

I never had a female role model, although the closest was Diane Jones Konihowski, the Saskatchewan pentathlete. I knew about her because Dad always talked about how great she was. I also followed the career of Martina Navratilova, the tennis player. I had no female role models in hockey. I wanted to be like Mark and Wayne.

Young girls now have role models and they have Olympic athletes to look up to. We are the role models. There was one young girl, about nine, a defenceman who plays hockey with the boys. She asked me to autograph her Team Canada jersey, and then she pointed to the jersey and said, "That's my spot right there. Someday, that's where my autograph is going to go."

Those are incredible moments, small but memorable things that happen over and over again. I met another girl at the rink after practice. She brought a goalie stick to get autographed. She said, "Hey, remember me? I came to Bear Mountain the last time you guys played here in Victoria, and you gave me a puck. I was one of the ones who hung around all the time." I did remember her. These moments make us realize the impact we can have as hockey players, that what we do can change someone's life.

WE PLAY THE U.S. TOMORROW. Looking back at the Canada Cup loss, I think we're almost a brand new team now: we have units, we have some systems, we know some roles, we have specialty teams, and we've got players who are more content with who they are and with what they're able to do on the ice. The Canada Cup was a bit of a free-for-all, we didn't have as much structure within our group, or confidence. Now, after some games against the Midgets, we do and we come into this game feeling great. But those games don't have the same meaning as Canada versus the U.S. There's just no way I can see the U.S. beating us. I see a lot of holes in their game, I see a lot of discipline in ours. There's a positive atmosphere and mood around our team now.

I'm feeling really good. Lately I've been playing with Agosta and Poulin, just trying to do good things, make them better players on the ice. Sometimes the consistency with young players isn't always there, but we've been pushing the envelope, playing with speed and poise, and that's positive.

I didn't practise with the team today. In Friday's 4-2 win in Red Deer, Agosta and I ran into each other, a knee to the head, and it scrambled my eggs a little bit. If I'm in the lineup tomorrow I'll play with Cherie Piper and Agosta. Piper and I played in the 2006 Games. She's a real smart, heads-up player who has struggled with injuries the last few years, but she's healthy now and in a good frame of mind. When she's on, she's an excellent hockey player, so I look forward to playing with her.

Who knows if this will be the lineup that we'll have when we play in the Olympic Games? The U.S. has been playing with mainly the same forward units the last while, playing college teams and beating them with scores like 13-0 and 6-1. We've been playing games against the guys and winning 2-1 and 4-2—good competitive, close games. Playing the Midget teams is giving us a competitive edge.

OCTOBER 15

You might say the game in Victoria was the TSN Turning Point so far in our season. We beat the U.S. 3-1! We had a different attitude in the dressing room, all about having nothing to lose, just take it to them instead of playing on our heels and playing tentative.

The crowd was phenomenal—6,100 people and lots of kids and families. Interestingly there were also older guys, true hockey guys, who probably have never seen women's hockey. After the game I heard that a lot of these men were saying, "Wow, these girls can really play hockey." When I hear those comments it makes me so proud of what we do. We're changing the old, traditional views and opinions of people.

You can't leave a game like that not loving what you saw, especially the end. Cherie Piper smoked Natalie Darwitz—she's the Americans' best player—just took her two feet off the ice with three and a half seconds left in the game. What ensued was a line brawl, a pushing and shoving match where every player on the ice, except Darwitz, ended up with a ten-minute misconduct. I was in there, it was my line that was on the ice. It was so much fun. I saw Angela Ruggiero, number 4, and went right for her. I always love to go at her.

Yes, we played with an attitude, as if to say: "You're in our country and you're in our Olympic province—you're not going to win." We had a great performance from goaltender Kim St-Pierre, we had timely goals, a good power-play goal to start. In general, players feel more comfortable now that we have systems, we have lines, we have some structure. Our team is probably 10 to 15 per cent improved from the Canada Cup in August.

Halfway through the third period, I jumped on to the ice and felt my knee twinge a bit. I don't know what caused it, but I had to get to the dressing room. Doug Stacey, our physio, quickly taped my knee. I was able to go back on the ice, not miss a shift, and finish the game. Dr. Diane Simpson, our team doctor, checked me out and said I should probably get a brace and have an MRI.

After the game we all went out as a team and had fun at a local watering hole. Even though we knew we had to get on the plane and bus at 6 AM the next day, it was a lot of laughs. We watched the TSN highlights, we were one of the big stories of the night. The commentators were saying, "Have you ever seen this in women's hockey?" Our team was cheering, screaming about it. It almost felt like we won the World Championships. We needed the win, to remember what it feels like to defeat the U.S.

WE FLEW HOME, AND I spent the rest of the day cleaning and organizing until Noah got home from school. I also went for an MRI. I was very nervous and very hopeful that nothing major had happened. I kept testing my knee throughout the day just to make sure it wasn't the medial collateral ligament, because that would mean I'd need a long time to heal. I saw Dr. Jim Thorne at our arena, and he said if it was major I'd be out for two to three weeks.

But the news was good. The MRI revealed that everything basically looks good, the ligaments are okay, there's just a bit of narrowing of my meniscus, which is the cushioning between the two leg bones. The narrowing can be offset with rehabilitation and strengthening exercises. If I can keep it stable, it's back to the weight room. If I miss three or four days of not keeping my legs strong, even though we're on the ice and skating all the time, I miss out on that strength, and it affects the tracking of my knee and the stability of my lower body. I have to get in there and keep doing those lower body exercises. I need to stay strong for the type of game I like to play, which is a hundred miles an hour, not taking a shift off, crash and bang if I have to. I'm thirty-one and I've got an old knee some days, but a young knee most days. I need to keep it that way.

I MISSED A 4-3 OVERTIME WIN in Calgary this week because I flew to Vancouver for the renaming of the UBC Thunderbird Arena, which will be called the Doug Mitchell Thunderbird Sports Centre, named after Doug and Lois Mitchell. They are good friends and have been great supporters of women's hockey. Doug is a former commissioner of the CFL, was on the board of governors for the NHL, and played for the B.C. Lions. He and his wife, Lois—she is a mentor to me—are big supporters of Canadian Interuniversity Sport, and of our team. During the Olympics, our team will be playing two games in that arena, so I felt it was important to represent our team and represent women's hockey at the celebration.

There was an on-ice presentation, hosted by Olympic broadcast legend Brian Williams, with a group of five-year-old kids. I wore my jersey and went on the ice, dropped the puck and played for five minutes with the kids. We then went upstairs for a sit-down dinner above the arena, and it was a Who's Who of Canadian Sport—the Minister of Sport, Chris Rudge of the Canadian Olympic Committee—plus a variety of presidents and CEOs of companies like CP Rail and Scotiabank. It was a great chance to meet and interact with people who are very successful.

Doug doesn't like recognition, but I think the night meant a lot to him. When you agree to raise and donate ten million dollars to an academic institution and you care for sport that much, it says a lot about who you are as a person and what you've accomplished in your life.

A BUSY DAY, but it was important for me to be there despite the extra travel and missed game. Noah wasn't too happy when he woke up on the day I left. I had moved his Lego machines so they weren't in the exact spot that he likes them. He proceeded to freak out, crying, "Why are you always leaving and why can't you stay home and not go to hockey ever again and not go to practice ever again and hang out with me?"

That, of course, was the real issue. It breaks my heart, it really does, every time I have to leave him. Sometimes it bothers him, sometimes it doesn't, but he's sensing his Mom is gone a lot. I miss him, too. I try not to be away for too many important events.

Off the ice, some days there are just too many things to manage. At times I feel overwhelmed, especially with the media and the extracurricular stuff. I'm going to have to get a better handle on all this as we move forward, because there is more and more coming at me every day. They might just be little requests: A newspaper wants you to call them; a TV station wants you to sit in studio for an interview; or can you come see this school? These things can start taking up two and three hours of a day. That's a lot of time, especially on a day off or when I might have only two or three hours to rest. It's up to me to manage that better and also to balance that with Noah's schedule and Tomas's schedule. Right now I'm fighting the schedule, the travel, the fatigue, not feeling totally rested every time I get on the ice.

SPEAKING OF TRAVEL, tonight we are in Spokane. Tomas drove me to the airport this morning. I walked through the front door of the airport and realized, "Holy shit! I forgot my passport!" This was after our coach had said many times to us, "Don't forget to bring your passports." This, after I have never forgotten my passport in all the years I have competed in sport. It's just a sign that there is too much on my personal conveyor belt right now. I borrowed Mel's truck, her keys, ripped out of the airport parkade, drove home, found my passport, turned around, and drove way too fast back to the airport. What a shit show!

We got on the plane, flew to Seattle, and had an hour's break before moving on to Spokane. We watched CNN footage of a little boy who apparently was trapped in a balloon high in the atmosphere. It turned out he was in a cardboard box in his parents' house in Colorado! That drama entertained us throughout the trip. It's just amazing what people will cover down here. It certainly captivated me, having a little boy and thinking, "Oh my God, there's a child up in the air." I'm tired and frazzled with a lot of things on my mind besides hockey. Noah heads off to Sweden tomorrow with Susan Nordean, our very good friend. I will miss him until I get there for the Four Nations Cup. I feel in need of a holiday in the middle of this Olympic centralization process.

Oh yes, and I saw they unveiled the Olympic medals. Fantastic. Very exciting. I'm looking forward to winning one—I just hope it's the right colour.

OCTOBER 18

Tomas and I went out for dinner and to a play last night, a rare occurrence. It's the first time in months we've actually gone out and done anything like that. Tomas loves the arts—opera, classical music. He was born in Prague. His father was a famous sports reporter who covered twelve Olympics, and Tomas had opportunities to travel extensively with him. And here I am, from a small town in Saskatchewan. Talk about two worlds colliding!

I enjoy getting away from the hockey rink, whether it's through music—orchestras or concerts—or theatre, just something different to stimulate the mind. The play was called 7 Stories, about a guy attempting to commit suicide on a balcony but all these people come out and try to convince him, indirectly, why he shouldn't. It's a comedy but there's a good message there about finding the little things to enjoy in life, not getting too serious about life. At times we all need to hear that message.

Noah is in Sweden—in Eskilstuna, which is where I played last season, and he is going to go to school there for a week. We wanted to send him back there to learn the language and see his friends again. It's important for a kid to have those opportunities. He doesn't have a typical life. He's travelled a lot since he was a small child, and we're often in and out of arenas, coming here and going there, with Olympics every few years. So he craves the normalcy of routine, but at the same time he also loves to travel. I've always wanted my kids to be citizens of the world and to be educated by the university of the world. Travel provides opportunities to learn things no classroom can teach.

We spoke to him this morning, and he hasn't missed us at all. Maybe when he's older he'll think, "Hey, my Mom wasn't normal, that's for sure. She was definitely weird, and different, sometimes annoying, neurotic, and obsessed with hockey. But at the same time she gave me a lot of opportunities to do interesting things."

His time in Sweden also gives me some space, some downtime which, selfishly, I look forward to. Tomas is on the road, back and forth from Camrose to Portland to Medicine Hat, working with individual players and teams. Our paths crisscross throughout the week. It's nice to worry about myself for a little while. I'm looking forward to going to Sweden and seeing Noah and Susan a couple days before the team arrives.

The team is in a good place right now. In Spokane we came out with guns a-blazing and defeated the U.S. 5-2. The crowd was decent, about 5,500, but the atmosphere was dead. I don't know if the U.S. players are tired but I can certainly see a shift since the Canada Cup. We've made a lot of progress as a team, especially in our fitness and conditioning. They just can't match our pace over sixty minutes. Our execution was good, our power play clicked. I moved up to the top on the power play. I've been hoping to play there for a long time, and it's just given the other four players more room on the ice. We've got Caroline Ouellette in the middle and the hole—she poses a threat with her quick, hard shot and size—with crafty Hefford and skilled Agosta and Vaillancourt down low. So we have five threats who can all handle the puck and do things with it. That's positive for our team, to have real confidence in this power play.

It was a great win. We're accustomed now to the tempo of the Midget AAA game. The Americans aren't playing that type of tempo. We step out on the ice and it's obvious. The momentum is shifting. We still have more games against the U.S. and we may not win them all, but every game now is a new script and a new chance to rewrite the story as we head into the Games. Forget that we lost the world championship. Play for the day.

The NHL Network covered the game live in the U.S. I texted Bobby Clarke and asked him to watch. He replied afterward to say he loved watching it and ask if we always played that type of attack game and if we always played that well. It was nice to get those comments.

After the game we came back to the hotel and changed, and pretty much the whole team went to a local restaurant. It was a chance to decompress as a group. We spend a lot of time throughout the week, and in the Midget games, just playing and resting, competing. When we get on the road, that's our chance to go out together—you don't have to worry about your kids, your family, getting home to things. I don't spend a lot of downtime with the team when I'm in Calgary, because I'm taking care of my son or other things. But on the road it's important—especially for me as a captain to go out and show the girls I'm a human being, have a beer every once in a while, laugh and tell jokes, show a side they may not have seen from me.

TOMORROW THE TEAM IS OFF to Grande Prairie. Ten hours on the bus. God help us! I am dreading it, absolutely dreading it. I do not like bus trips. We have three games this week against Midget teams, a team-building weekend then we fly to Europe.

I'm going out for Vietnamese food tonight with some friends. Tomas is at the Portland-Calgary Western Hockey League game. Somewhere, Noah is eating Swedish meatballs and loving every second of the fact that he can have the world at his fingertips.

OCTOBER 23

It's hard to believe that as an Olympic team training for an Olympics in our home country we still have to sit on a bus for ten hours to go play a game. But it's what we do.

That said, I prefer the bus over flying because going up and down in the air is really hard on the body. I'm less fatigued getting off a bus than I am an airplane. Air travel induces physiological changes—it dehydrates you, pools the blood in your legs; you tend to sit in one spot and not move around. On the bus, for the most part, we get our own seats. I'll often lie down and put my legs up on the window.

I'm not sure if it's the same for all teams, but our team definitely has a "bus culture." There are players who like to play cards and visit. They generally sit at the back. Then there's the group that's into computers and video games. They sit in the middle. The quieter group, people who like to sleep, sits at the front. I like to sit at the front—five rows back, on the right-hand side. That's probably the only superstition I have.

Our road trip started with a game against Grande Prairie, which we won 5-1. I find these Midget games difficult at times. I've been playing against these boys, who are sixteen and seventeen years old, since I was their age, and some days I have to change my routine and find extra motivation to get up for the game. That usually means I warm up harder by doing more sprints, or if it's forty-below I warm up outside to force myself to wake up. I push my body a little harder to wake up and feel the burn or pain before I get on the ice. Most of our players are Midget-sized players with Junior A or better skill levels. It's just the size factor that prevents us from playing the next level of hockey, more than it is reading the game or skill.

Next morning we moved on to Edmonton. I thought we were playing in Spruce Grove. I kept asking the girls, "When are we going to be in Spruce Grove?" And they'd say, "We're not going to Spruce Grove, we're going to Edmonton." Sometimes I lose complete track of what day it is, what time it is, and who we are playing. Tell me to get on the bus, tell me when the meal is, tell me when the game is, and I'll take care of everything else because nothing else really matters. Teams, games—they're all sort of the same. The girls were ripping me for being a space cadet. But the fact is I don't remember much. Maybe it's because I took a big hit last year in Sweden, or I'm under stress or whatever. I forget things a lot, except for the important things. It's like we have this conveyer belt in our brains, it will only hold so much and if it isn't important or useful it falls right off, never to be found again. It seems to happen to me a lot. At least I gave them all something to laugh about.

We played in Edmonton and won 3–0, although I missed a breakaway and that really pissed me off. I didn't get home until 4 AM, a very short morning because I had to get up and do a campaign for Plan Canada's "Because I Am a Girl" program. It's about empowering girls and women around the world. There are a billion people living below the poverty line in this world, and 70 per cent are female. In most of these developing countries women are heading households and working jobs and are really the cornerstones of their families. Giving them greater opportunities provides their kids and everyone in their communities a chance for a better life. That's a very good thing.

Afterward I came home, had a nap, and drove to Strathmore. The game was a disaster. We lost 6–0. Our fatigue level was obvious. It was our worst showing of the season. Carla MacLeod got absolutely trampolined through the air—a small girl hits a big boy, and that's what happens. But I almost felt our coaching staff set us up to not be successful because we had been on a good run with the Midget teams. Sometimes coaches hope the team has setbacks, adversity, just so players don't become complacent. At least, it appeared that way to me. We had different lines, different power play units. It annoys me a bit because as a player you play every game to win, and players don't like change. Knowing our team and the type of team we were facing, it seemed like bad timing to be making changes. But something told me there was a method behind the madness, and I let it go at that.

OCTOBER 25

We had a team-building workshop this weekend. They had us do the TAIS, and let me tell you, it is one of the most awful things to do. However, it's very good for feedback and personal analysis. But when you're tired and you've been on the road for a week, it's probably the last thing you want to do—sit in a conference room with your teammates and tell them all about yourself and all your strengths and all your weaknesses. It's tough, and for me it's awkward.

TAIS stands for The Attention and Interpersonal Style inventory. It is used in business, sport, and military organizations. It is supposed to reveal how pressure affects our motivation and our ability to concentrate and communicate. The exercise is meant to help us improve decision-making, mental, and interpersonal skills.

It was very interesting. I looked back over my scores from the last Olympics and from 2002. My decision-making style went from 21 per cent to 62 per cent, meaning I am better at making decisions and not as likely to "wishy-wash" as I was in the past. My self-confidence went down—which probably just means maturity. As you get older you don't think you're quite as invincible, you're more realistic about the world.

My "expression of support and affection" actually went down, which means I'm less likely to express support and affection. I don't need a lot of that positive stuff, so I don't naturally give it out. That is an interesting revelation, given I'm the team captain. What else? Ah, self-critical. I was almost 100 per cent self-critical.

We then had to write about ourselves and read it to our teammates. Horrifying, you might think. And it was. But I managed to write it in twenty minutes, and I think I was fairly accurate. "I have a flexible style," I wrote, "and a personality that can be hard to read. I have a dependable work ethic. I tend toward perfectionism but I can handle volume with lots going on around me. The challenge for me is to understand others who don't have that capacity.

"I like to lead and I enjoy people, but I find being a cheerleader to be draining. I am equally extroverted and introverted and need my own space to recharge my batteries. I learned at a young age not to listen to the critical opinion of others, which was how I survived many difficult situations. I need to lighten up at times and enjoy the moment more. For example, when we win a gold medal and stand on the blue line to celebrate, I am already thinking: "Oh my God, we have to do this again in four more years."

"In most situations I will have to tell others what I like about them and express my confidence in them, as that is what they want. I feel like a long branch on a tree—the one that has been around a long time and has seen it all, the one everyone wants to play on, climb on, swing on, and trim down; it enjoys the action and has the strength to handle it. But if it doesn't get proper food, water, and rest it might break off."

That is how I described myself. I read it to my best friend, Danielle Greenberg, tonight, and she laughed her head off, saying, "That's exactly you!"

They also gave us some team feedback. Here are the overall attributes of our team: "The key attribute is that the group shares a desire to play well and win. There is a great deal of inner drive, strong determination, and a push to constantly raise the bar. This team expends a huge amount of energy on the ice and in their heads. They need to be careful they use the energy on what will be of most benefit. Strong and well-disciplined, they can get tentative when the pressure is on."

We had to go around the room and decide what we feel are our biggest team strength and biggest team weakness. We decided the strength was competitiveness and the challenge was confidence. We have to celebrate one another's successes and learn when to build people up.

We went on to have dinner at Hockey Canada president Bob Nicholson's house. There, we were presented with money from the TELUS Going for Gold golf tournament held at the Red Tail course near London, Ontario. Each player received a cheque for ten thousand dollars. Some of the girls cried, some were well and truly taken aback. It is a lot of money. It shows the athletes that people care. Bob and his wife, Lorna, hosted the evening. Bob has gone to bat for us for many years, and he genuinely cares. It's important to acknowledge that, because he has a tough job and a big job. He's got a good heart.

I miss Noah. He's been in Sweden for the past week and loving life—having sleepovers at his friend Per's house, going to school, going to museums, and being a little Swedish boy.

NOVEMBER 3

We are now in Finland for the Four Nations Cup. It's interesting being back in this part of the world. I played in Sweden in 2008–09, and before this tournament I arrived in Stockholm ahead of our team to spend some time with Noah and Susan before they travelled back to Canada.

Noah's Swedish classmates treated him beautifully. They had a Halloween party for him, something they don't normally do in this part of the world. At the same time he was able to work on his Swedish and being comfortable in another country. Noah could have stayed a bit longer but he wanted to be home for Halloween. So even though we parted he was happy, because he arrived home in time for his jelly bean dance and his Halloween party.

After the team arrived we had an exhibition game against Sweden in Stockholm. Our first period was pathetic. It was actually nice to see the Swedes—they had about a thousand, maybe 1,500 people at the game, and probably would have had more except it conflicted with the largest soccer game to be held in Sweden in twenty years, with Stockholm AIK playing the Gothenburg team. Ten years ago there would have been fifty people in the rink so the women's game has come a long way here. After a slow start we picked it up in the second and third periods. I was playing with Poulin and Piper. We ended up winning 4–2 although the Swedes led for most of the game and were up 2–1 heading into the third period. It was a tough game to win but we managed to pull it out with our power play, and I got the winner late in the third period. Then they folded.

While in Stockholm I also had an opportunity to watch an Elite League game with some of our staff—Djurgårdens versus Timrå. None of the other girls wanted to go, but because I've lived over here I have an interest in watching it. I always learn something from international hockey and enjoy watching some of the young NHL draft picks. You can also learn about the hockey style of an opponent you're about to play—why they do what they do. Playing in Sweden last year, playing that trap style every day, it was frustrating to have to play that patient game. It's almost a game of chess on ice. But by watching, you learn how you can play against it; you learn why a system like that works and how to beat it. They could improve their game by miles if they played more of a pressure style, more forechecking, more hitting, but maybe that's a secret we Canadians have that keeps us successful.

WE'RE STAYING AT A Finnish training centre called Vierumäki. It's interesting to be back in Finland, having played here professionally several years ago. I lived and played in Sweden last year, and there is a real difference between the two countries. Sweden is an easier country to live in, a nicer lifestyle, more money. When I'm in Finland I feel like I'm in the middle of Russia. It's a little depressed, the architecture isn't quite as elaborate, life isn't quite as affluent as it is in Sweden. That being said, living in Finland was one of the best episodes in my life because of the friends I made and the experiences I had.

When we arrived in Vierumäki, the girls complained about it being dark here at four in the afternoon and the food being so bad. I just laughed and said, "I lived with that for eight months here, by myself. I had no family and no friends to begin with, and now I have great friends here." Becky Kellar looked at me and said, "I don't know how you did it."

I don't know that I could do it again by myself. At times you're ready for things in your life and you do them because you can handle them. I lived and played in Sweden last season, and Tomas and Noah were with me. It was possible because I had my family there.

But I look back at all the things I went through here in Finland by myself: playing in terrible arenas, surrounded by a language I don't speak, food I don't normally eat, people I don't know; isolation; depression; no daylight; grey skies; winning, losing, playing well, not playing well, getting ice time, not getting ice time. I have been through it all. Unfortunately, I didn't get an opportunity to share that with my teammates or any other people in my life at the time because I did it by myself. It was such a unique, stressful, exciting time of my life.

Vierumäki has great facilities but it is in the middle of the forest. It is very dark, and there is absolutely nothing to do, which, for an elite athlete, is a great thing. Some of the girls are looking for the mall, the stores, movie theatres. They are far, far away from this place. We are in a dorm, a very modern dorm with a microwave and a nice TV and a sink and a fridge, a shower and a comfortable bed. It certainly isn't the worst place I've stayed in. The food isn't the worst I've eaten but it isn't the best—beet salad, boiled potatoes, some sort of fish or meat every day with cucumbers and tomatoes, and not many other choices. And the arena is nothing special. I'm disappointed we play two games of the tournament here because there is seating for about one hundred people. It's really just a training rink.

Tonight we began the Four Nations tournament with a 4–0 win against Sweden. We played much better than we did in an exhibition game a couple of days ago. But there were maybe forty people in the rink, no atmosphere.

After doing this for sixteen years, I have to find ways to keep myself on my toes, mix it up. I said to Ryan van Asten, our strength and conditioning coach, "I'm struggling today. We have to do something to wake up here. This is just not exciting." We did a vigorous warm-up outside in the cold air, followed by some agility stuff. I just tried to wake my body up physically and find a way to get my head into the game. As it turned out, I played pretty well.

NOVEMBER 7

Each game serves as a learning experience for us as we move forward in this pre-Olympic schedule. Earlier this week we played Finland and won 4–2 even though at one point they went ahead of us 2–1. Right now we tend to excel in the third period, we're able to wear teams down with our fitness, our skating, and our finish. I'm not so sure we're ready to go off the drop.

The Finns play a scrappy, annoying, in-your-face, trapping, clog-up-the-neutral-zone style. They work hard. They want to battle. They aren't skilful or fit enough to go the distance with us, but they have improved. They have a respectable guy behind the bench; he coached their world junior men's team a few years ago. It's not a gimme when you play Sweden or Finland. It's actually a scary movie sometimes because you don't know what you're going to get. Their brand of hockey is so unpredictable. Playing them is like a dance but you don't know what your dance partner is going to do. That's why at the Olympics, or any tournament, we can't afford to take any team for granted.

People say this is only a two-team tournament, but we know that Sweden and Finland can be dangerous. Anything can happen. You get a penalty, they get an early goal, you get tight, they get great goaltending, you get in trouble.

The Americans beat us 3–2 in the third round robin game of the tournament. It was a sloppy affair. We couldn't score, we had power play chances that just didn't work very well. To their credit, the USA had made some adjustments from the last time we played them, and played more aggressively. We still outplayed them and out-chanced them but just couldn't score. Needless to say, we were looking forward to getting out of Vierumäki and out of that environment of no sun, no atmosphere, bad food.

WE MET THE U.S. tonight in the Four Nations gold medal final in Tikkurila, a suburb of Helsinki. It brought back a lot of memories for me, as the game was in the same arena where I played the last game of my last year in Finland.

I had played a number of games through the season—I think I had four points in seven games in the Mestis, the second-highest level of the Finnish League. Our team, HC Salamat, had won the year before to move up to the Mestis. We were about ten games into the season, and I hadn't been getting much ice time from the coach, Matti Hagman. It was clear he didn't want me around. I said to him the night before the game in Tikkurila, "If you're not going to play me, don't dress me. It's better for me, it's embarrassing for me to be on the bench all game and not take a shift." He said, "No, I'm going to play you. You'll dress."

So I dressed. First period goes by, second period goes by—not a second of ice time. By that point the fans were starting to get anxious. The building was full. The crowd started chanting: "Hayley, Hayley." The people of Finland were so nice to me, gracious even in buildings that were not my home arena. I think they were intrigued with a woman playing professional men's hockey.

The pressure from the crowd, or something, finally got to Hagman, and he threw me out on the ice for a mercy shift later in the third period. I was pretty angry by that point, so I threw it back in his face. I skated up the ice, down the ice, lasted about fifteen seconds on the ice and came right back off and sat at the end of the bench—kind of a Screw You moment. The next day I decided it wasn't going to work out for me. I was lonely and homesick, and it just wasn't worth it for me anymore. So the last game I played was in that building.

FAST-FORWARD TO TONIGHT: the Four Nations final. It was awesome. We played well and we won 5–1. The power play worked, we had great secondary scoring. More than anything, the feeling has really changed within our team. We've put some doubt into the U.S. At this point we're the better team. I truly believe that. We have better depth line for line, and our top players are better. Their goaltending has not been outstanding, and ours has been solid.

It was a great win, but businesslike. The girls pumped fists and high-fived the goalie, but there was no great celebration. It was the Four Nations Cup, and we knew it was important just for the confidence of our group. We hugged goalie Shannon Szabados, I was happy for her to get the win and to beat the U.S. in a tournament. We received a little Finnish wooden plaque as tournament winner—it was the map of Finland, the cheesiest thing you have ever seen. We calmly shook hands, got off the ice, and went about our business with no great fanfare or speeches. We undressed with the attitude of, "We took care of that!"

Winning the tournament was a relief more than anything, as most of the wins usually are for me. I always feel a sense of relief, not a sense of joy—maybe because it's always expected. Overall, it was a very good tournament. I had one goal and six assists, or something like that. I didn't score a lot but I made things happen, I was happy with my play. This team is really making strides, and I take pride in that.

TRIUMPHS AND
TRIBULATIONS

NOVEMBER 16

After the Four Nations Cup we had a week off, and today was our first day back at the rink. I was there from about 8 AM to 5:30 PM—from eight to one o'clock I was involved with the Wayne Gretzky Samsung kids' event. The fifteen kids in attendance had a variety of stories—some had lost siblings, there was one whose mother had cancer, some were chosen just for their love of the game and the crazy things they do to play and be around hockey.

It was a fun day for the kids and for me, too. It's amazing how much media shows up when Wayne is on the ice. I don't envy his life at times. Every media outlet in Calgary was there, everyone was intrigued by him, as usual.

There were probably a hundred people standing on the bench watching the clinic—parents and media and Hockey Canada staff, just wanting to get a glimpse of the Great One. It's funny how life has come full circle for me. I grew up admiring Wayne Gretzky, and there I was hanging out in the dressing room chatting with him before going out on the ice, sharing the same ice surface, doing the same things. As a kid I never would have thought that would happen for me. Yesterday was a unique experience. It was great to see the smiles on the kids.

Wayne also came to our dressing room and said hello to the team for a couple of minutes. He asked how the year was going and wished us good luck. After he left, we had a quick meeting. Everyone was chatty, talking about their holidays, where they went for their week off, excited to get back to work. We went for a quick weight workout, played volleyball, then hit the ice for a two-hour practice. I don't know why they had to have a two-hour practice after a week off. Just in case we missed everything? It would have been good to have an hour, hard, and get off the ice. We play a lot of games this week, three games. But nope, we have to be out there for two hours, which doesn't make any sense to me. But that's why I'm not coaching, I'm just a player.

Tomas and I both have crazy schedules this week. We're constantly juggling, that's probably the hardest thing at this point—making sure we're spending enough time with Noah, picking him up, getting everything going. He competed in a swim meet last week and did really well: he finished in the top five in all his races but was disqualified in his breaststroke. It's weird being a parent and just sitting, watching. Tomas and Mom were cheering on both sides of me and in the middle I was totally calm, watching Noah and laughing. I don't feel any pressure for him, not yet anyway. I'm probably the most laid-back parent there is, which is a sharp contrast to who I am as an athlete. Afterward I asked him if he was proud of himself, and he said, "Yeah." That's all that matters.

A long week and more games loom ahead. I received a nice e-mail from Mark Messier. He talked about how there is no failure, the focus has to be on me being a consistent and transparent leader every day, with a perspective of just doing what I do and feeling the joy of it.

NOVEMBER 21

It's been hectic with three Midget AAA games this week, more meet-and-greets and a fair bit of drama in the mix when we played the South Side Athletic Club team in Edmonton.

What ensued would be the "Phaneuf Incident" for anyone who might have seen it on TSN. It was a crazy game, on a shoebox-sized ice surface, that started in the warm-up with one of their guys skating by me saying, "I'll be in your grill all night, Hayley." Trash-talking!

I've played Midget AAA players since I was a Midget AAA fifteen years ago—I've played hundreds of games against these guys. Honestly, I'd have to say this was probably the worst experience I've had with a team. They didn't seem too excited about playing us because the game didn't allow hitting. All they did, all game long, was yap, yap, yap—especially at me. I'm not sure what the other girls heard but I heard some outrageous stuff, from being called Hamburger Helper to probably the worst things that could be said to a woman.

What did we do? We played sixty minutes of good hockey. Thank God, we beat them 6-1. Our goaltender, Szabados, stood on her head and won the game for us, and our power play worked well.

They were a good team, big boys, probably bigger on average than most Midget teams in the league. Half of their team must have been six feet tall, maybe 180-plus pounds. This was actually one of the few games where I was worried for some of our smaller players. I felt safer playing professional men's hockey because those guys could control their bodies, they were not going to take liberties that can end your career. Midget teams, they're sixteen years old, hormones going everywhere, and if they make one hit not looking the right way, well that can end your career. I felt they took a lot of liberties on our small players, and head shots on everyone. There were cheap shots off the face-off, absolutely outrageous, on top of talking, talking, talking all game long and really being very rude.

It's one thing to play physical, play hard, which we of course always want to do. If you get knocked down, whatever, penalties happen. That's fine. I don't snap often, maybe out of sixty games it might happen two or three times. Well, in the last minute

Dane Phaneuf—younger brother of Dion, who plays for the Calgary Flames—rubbed me out, bumped, hit me, whatever you want to call it, behind the net. It was definitely a penalty. It wasn't a dirty hit or anything. He was basically in the wrong place at the wrong time, took a penalty at the wrong time, and I didn't like it very much. By that point I had had enough. I skated over to him and put him in a headlock.

It doesn't look very good, a thirty-one-year-old fighting a fifteen-year-old. But I had to stand up not only for myself but also for my teammates, who had just been taking it all game long. Nothing really came out of it other than television was there filming the game. Of course, because his last name is Phaneuf and I'm who I am, it ended up on TSN. I'm sure there were lots of comments on how it should have been handled, what I should have done, and what he should have done.

I had expected TSN to follow up with it. I was told they were coming to the rink the next night to talk about it, but they never showed up. It's good to see it all blow over because it was really nothing—it was a harmless play in a game that was out of control at times. But we handled ourselves well as a team. That's hockey: it's an emotional game, and you have to stand up for yourself and your teammates. Sometimes the girls have a hard time against the boys because they can't physically match their strength or size so they don't really know what to do. There are times you just have to put yourself out there and see what happens. Physically, I'm able to do that so that's what I did. We had a few laughs about it after the game, it was no big deal. The media tried to make it bigger than it was.

The thing that irks me, and a lot of the girls were pissed off about it, is that TV was there for the whole game. We kicked butt, 6-1, and the only thing they showed was a highlight of one goal and then talked about my little incident for twenty-five seconds.

They didn't talk about any of the skilful goals, of which there were many; or the great saves; or how Caroline Ouellette dangled through their whole team to score a highlight reel goal. They never show any highlights from other games except when we play the U.S., and even then only if it's a scuffle or a fight after the game. Very rarely do they follow with in-depth coverage.

It's disheartening that sometimes the only way we can get coverage is when something stupid like that happens. A lot of my teammates were upset about it. I talked to them about it after and said, "That's the media, always looking for an angle." God forbid they follow us for a three-game series and see what it's actually like, day in and day out, to play these guys, the size disadvantages that we have. Yet we still find ways to win games and play skilful hockey.

At times we're in a lose-lose situation when we play these Midget games. If we win, people say, "Yeah, well, it's just the Midget AAAs." If we lose, we get "Hey, the women's national team can't even beat a Midget AAA team." It's a tough thing.

We try to find games to match our skill, our size. Playing junior is the next step, and we get that chance in December, when we play the Junior A, Tier Two Canucks in Calgary. It's a big moment for us.

There was a time when we'd only win 50 per cent of these Midget games. This season I think we're going to win 80 per cent or more. Our record will show that we can play night in and night out.

NOVEMBER 27

I was a bit under the weather all this week—I missed practice on Monday and our game on Tuesday, which we won 4-3. I practised on Wednesday and then we played Thursday night, losing our fourth game of the season in the Midget AAA series, 4-3. At one point we were down 3-0. We battled back to get to a pretty good spot, but we just couldn't find the handle to get the winner. I scored one of my nicest goals of the season.

Tomas came to the game. He doesn't get to watch too many this season because of his travel. He told me I don't play with any fire. Watching my body language, he says I'm thinking too much out on the ice. His opinion matters because he knows the game and the players better than most. He's pretty fair in evaluating my play, and if he says I need to get better, then I probably do. That's caused me to watch videos of the last few games and evaluate myself and my body language and what I'm doing.

I need to shoot more, take the puck to the net, get into the traffic, and try a little more stuff one-on-one. In my own defence, I was probably playing with one lung, I couldn't breathe very well. I felt like I was hyperventilating the whole game, I couldn't seem to catch my breath. My heart rate was pretty high, not surprising as I've been fighting something. With our travel and fatigue level, the immune system gets compromised. I usually choose not to get the flu shot, just to let my body naturally heal. Lemon tea. Hot water. Cold-FX. Vitamin C. Sleep—a lot of sleep—and eating well. This is usually how I recover. Illness is very rare for me, and this recent one was nothing major. I wake up in the morning and cough out a couple of green chunks, then I'm good for the day. I know it's disgusting, but that's what it's like right now.

I HAD A CHAT WITH MEL. As team captain, it's important to touch base and get a feel for where the coach is coming from. My concerns were about how we are playing, the fatigue level, confirming her plans so I can relay that information back to the players. Since our week off, we have played five games in two weeks. I sense a pretty high level of fatigue and illness within our group, myself included. So I just touched base, found we are on the same page with everything. Away we went, had a short practice, forty minutes of flow, kind of a fun one, and called it a week.

They have cut Jocelyne Larocque and Brianne Jenner. We've been together in this centralization process since mid-August so it's tough to see anyone leave the group. But they have to eventually get the roster down to twenty-one—with these cuts we're down to twenty-four, so there's more coming. But these are two good, young players who will still get a chance with the under-22 group this season, and on the national team in the future.

NOVEMBER 30

Grey Cup is big wherever the game is held, and Calgary put on a great show this past weekend! It was Montreal versus Saskatchewan, and it was Go Riders Go in our house. Grey Cup was always a big thing for us when we lived in Shaunavon; Mom and Dad always had a party. I am a CFL fan. I still remember 1989, when Dave Ridgway kicked a field goal for the Riders to win the Grey Cup. We had quite the party back then! For me this past weekend was a chance to think about something other than hockey, if only for a day or two.

On Saturday night I met my Saskatchewan buddies, Carol Scheibel and Kelly Bechard, at "Riderville," part of the Grey Cup festivities here. It was like a typical Saskatchewan wedding. There were grandmas and grandpas out on the dance floor, bustin' it to AC/DC with the twenty-year-olds; people in their acid-wash jeans and their runners like right out of *Corner Gas.* It was so typically Saskatchewan, it just made me howl. There's something about the prairies and the people there that is so down to earth yet so damn crazy. People had Pilsner boxes on their heads, crazy hair, Santa and his elves were running around, fifty-something business people were just losing their minds for the weekend, completely getting their Green on, doing the Rider Pride thing.

On Sunday I donned my green Riders jacket and went to the game with Noah, his friend Isaac, and Carol. I've always said the

Grey Cup isn't a game, it's an event, and that's exactly what it turned out to be. It was amazing to see all the green, all the people who came from Saskatchewan. We had great seats in Row 1, right behind the uprights in the northwest end, where Montreal would eventually kick that field goal to win 28–27.

It was a beautiful day, and it stayed beautiful, it wasn't cold, and it was so special to be in the stands to see the event live. You see things you don't see on TV and you feel the emotion, you're part of it. I haven't actually watched many major sporting events live. But I said to Carol, "I could really become a fan of these big events because they get your adrenalin going!"

Saskatchewan started out great, and as the game progressed they slowly let Montreal back in, let them get their momentum. I could feel it coming. This Grey Cup will probably go down as the most exciting, crazy ending to a Grey Cup or any sport event. Montreal missed a field goal on their last play of the game but Saskatchewan had too many players on the field. To have thirteen men on the field—you're only allowed twelve—there was obviously a miscommunication. Montreal kicker Damon Duval missed the field goal. He is one of the best kickers in the league and, getting a second chance, I just knew he wasn't going to miss again.

It was interesting to watch the Riders the first time he kicked and missed. They were jumping all over the field, so excited thinking they'd won the game, until the orange flags went up. Some of the guys then fell to their knees, crumpled to the ground. They could not believe what had just happened. Duval had a second chance to kick, and everyone in the stadium knew he wasn't going to miss. McMahon Stadium was dead silent because it was pretty much full of Rider fans.

What a day, jubilation then letdown. It's tough being a fan because you have no control over what's going on out there. You're totally helpless. It's much better to play. As we walked out of the stadium, I said to Carol, "I never want to feel this way again. It felt the same as it did in 1998 when we lost the Olympic gold medal."

TODAY AT PRACTICE Mel wanted to have a moment to discuss the Grey Cup game. It was a real teaching moment and served as an important lesson for our team by reinforcing the saying that a game isn't over until it's over. What struck me was the amazing shift in momentum, and the ability of the Montreal offensive line to hang in there and give quarterback Anthony Calvillo the chance to get himself going, the way they stuck to the game plan. Meantime, Saskatchewan was playing not to lose instead of pushing the pace and trying to win.

As an athlete I believe it's always better to be on the attack than on the defence. Safe is Death. The Riders were a little too safe at the end, and it cost them. It reinforced my belief that you have to go for it and you never know what moment can change the course of a game. Montreal didn't deserve to win that game but, based on their record throughout the season, they had a terrific team and they knew it. They stayed confident.

It was great how our coaching staff acknowledged that. Every single player who watched that game saw, and took, teachable moments. Going into Vancouver and the Olympics, it doesn't matter if we are the underdog or the favourite. It's preparation, mindset, and how we handle ourselves in those sixty game minutes that will determine the outcome.

Tonight we're on our way to Red Deer—four games in seven days coming up. There's lots of hockey to be played.

DECEMBER 10

We're definitely heading in the right direction! In October we lost 6-0 to the UFA Bisons in Strathmore. On Monday night we played them again at Father Bauer and beat them 3-1.

Earlier this week we also enjoyed a major milestone when we played a Junior A team, the Calgary Canucks. Mel has worked as an assistant coach with that team. It was our first foray into Junior A hockey. Eight years ago we started to play the Midget AAAs and had to sneak away to Red Deer just to get a game, in obscurity, with these teams. Nobody thought we'd ever beat them.

Well, we beat those Junior A Canucks, 3–2. We played quite a good game. Shannon Szabados, our goaltender, faced fifty-four shots and stopped all but two. We had about twenty-five quality chances, and we put some in the net. This was a big moment for me. For people to see us beat Midget AAA teams is one thing. But when you beat the Junior As you're at a new respect level.

The biggest difference is the size of the players and the reach. And when they play us they can't hit so they don't truly get to play the physical style they are accustomed to, so it's not always a fair game. So kudos to them. But they also didn't know how to react to us, how to play us in the first two periods, and we snuck away with it. In the third period they pressured hard but we held on for the win.

I feel really good about the game and how our team played. I feel like I'm playing as well as I can at this point, although I could put the puck in the net more. It was a nice win on a night that was minus-25 in Calgary with an unbelievable snowfall. There are four-to five-foot snowdrifts everywhere; it's very cold, the biting cold of winter. Christmastime is looming, and I'm a bit tired, looking for a break. Our team has sucked it up in the last few games to get these wins, it's been really positive.

ON THE DOWNSIDE, defenceman Delaney Collins has been released. She'd been trying to make the Games for years—three Olympic attempts and she never made the team, although she made some world championship teams. Last year she suffered a concussion that kept her off the ice for almost a year. It was an amazing come-back just for her to get this far. She came into the dressing room in shock. She said she was released, she was cut, then just walked out. My heart sank for her.

Everyone was in a funk for the rest of the day. Some of the girls who were closer to her were very upset. There's her room-mate, Meghan Agosta, a young kid who now has to deal with her roommate being released and she is still trying to perform on the team. I went over and tried to comfort her. There's not much you can say. I left the rink in a sombre mood. Everybody knows cuts are going to be made, and you think you're prepared for it but you're not.

Wednesday we had to wake up and carry on. We had a team event planned in conjunction with the Toy Mountain campaign—the Salvation Army collects toys and gives them to less fortunate kids at Christmas. We had to shop for families who sent in lists, then put their gift bags together.

It was a joyous atmosphere, but with a serious undertone because Delaney was cut and more cuts are looming. It's tough on the players and it's tough on our coaching staff. I know it weighs heavily on Mel and the others who have to make those decisions. I don't envy the job.

But being at the Salvation Army, doing something for charity and the city, brings us together as a team. It humbles me. I look at the lists—some people have four kids, they all need things. These families arrive on a bus, maybe they don't have transportation to pick up Christmas gifts. You're going shelf by shelf, and you realize how generous people are to donate things, and also realize how much people need. As an athlete, these activities inject you with a dose of humility and perspective. After making another cut, it was not a bad plan by our coaches to take everybody back to reality here, to make us realize how at the end of the day it's just sport.

AFTERWARD, A FEW OF US went to Earl's for lunch. We chatted about the cuts. Then we chatted about Tiger Woods and his romantic misadventures. What a disaster! But I'm not going to judge a story that I read through speculation in the papers. What he did was wrong, but the other side of it is that we don't know what goes on, the media distorts and sensationalizes a lot of it. When you're in the public eye you have to make sure you take care of yourself, handle your image and your responsibilities well—because if you make a mistake the fallout is unrelenting. Not everyone feels they can be totally themselves in the public eye, because people are watching. You're always on guard.

The only responsibility you have is to yourself, your teammates, and the people around you. If you can be responsible to those people, that is good enough. If you try to satisfy the public by living up to some image or expectation, you will always fail. You never live up to that. But we are role models—just by doing what we love, training and striving to achieve something, having a goal and joy and purpose is very meaningful to young kids. As a kid you put athletes on a pedestal, but when you grow up you realize they're just human. We're all flawed. We all make mistakes.

After lunch it was back to the rink for a hard hour-and-a-half skate. Then I had to do some teasers for TSN and a couple of interviews with the Canadian Press about the climate change letter that twenty of us athletes sent to Prime Minister Stephen Harper in support of Play It Cool, a David Suzuki Foundation program. I did another interview about the upcoming game against the U.S. here in Calgary next week.

I cooled down, packed up my stuff, headed home, did some laundry, recycling, packed for our next road trip, picked up Noah at his friend's house and got a pizza—I didn't feel like cooking. I thought he needed to have a fun night with his Mom because I've been away a fair bit. We made a gingerbread house—a crazy gingerbread house with Lego characters and a *Twilight* theme because he recently watched the movie. We also watched *Dog the Bounty Hunter,* our current favourite show. Hilarious.

Our team is off to Denver to play the U.S. The last cuts will happen before Christmas. I look forward to getting our team settled and everybody going into Christmas break feeling good about themselves and the team. We're improving. I can see it day by day. I see the little things that we're doing, I see the habits, the demands being made on us, and we're meeting them, living up to them despite fighting through fatigue. We can't get comfortable or complacent even though we're having good success against the Midget teams. I know we're playing against better competition that anyone else. We're training at a higher level. We just need to trust and rest easy in that.

DECEMBER 15

Two more games against the U.S., and two more wins for Canada.

We played the Americans in Denver earlier this week and won 4-2 in front of a disappointing crowd of only a few thousand. The U.S. did not look good. They seemed to be struggling on their defence, they made a lot of mistakes. They ended up putting forwards, such as Julie Chu, on defence. She's a solid, veteran forward but they put her on defence! They had veteran Jessie Vetter, their number one goalie, in the net, and we got to her early. Other than that it was an uneventful game, no fights or anything out of the ordinary. It was an interesting momentum swing for us. After the game the U.S. and Canada players were standing as a group in the media area, and we could see the dejection on the Americans' faces. Our group is gaining confidence and momentum.

We came back to Calgary and played tonight in the Saddledome, a 6-2 win for us, but a disappointing game in terms of coverage and fan support. In 1998 when we played at the 'Dome we filled the building to capacity. Sold out. Rockin'. Great media. Fantastic exposure. It was a real boost for women's hockey, despite our losing that game 3–1. This time around, two months before the Olympics come to Canada, we had ten thousand people at the game. They had tried to sell a three-game package with the World Juniors, us, and the sledge hockey team, and they didn't release single-game tickets until four days before the game. Really disappointing. The city media was slow to pick it up—Mix 97.7 radio was the only one giving it good coverage, they were really pumping it. It was deflating. I tried not to let it bother me in the game, but on a personal note, to have lived in Calgary for pretty much the last twenty years, to step on the ice and see the Saddledome maybe half full when the Olympics are so close... well, that was disappointing.

Maybe it's a sign of the times in terms of the state of the women's game. In 1998 we were preparing for our first Olympics, and there was a novelty factor. Now people have seen Canada and the U.S. over and over and over. There's no shortage of excitement, they're great games to watch. But perhaps they're tired of always seeing Canada versus the U.S.

Enough of being Debbie Downer! The actual game was great for us. This team is proving time and again that it doesn't matter if we're up, down—whatever is going on in the game, we have the ability to come back and we have great firepower. The pulse and heartbeat of our game comes down to great goaltending, and if our defence just moves the puck simply we are usually okay. If our D struggles in our own end, if we struggle coming back and moving the puck up the ice, then we're in trouble.

After the game I walked by the American team's dressing room and saw their assistant coach just staring into space. The head coach, Mark Johnson, was talking to their strength trainer, probably saying, "How come these girls are getting outskated, and how come they are getting physically out-battled?"

1 Keeping cool while warming up—
Gillian Apps, Meghan Agosta, Caroline
Ouellette, and Hayley at boot camp
in Dawson Creek.

4

2 Governor General Michaëlle Jean takes
   the face-off in the athletes' village.

3 Retired NHL superstar Mark Messier
   shares advice, encouragement, and his
   birthday cake with Hayley and her
   teammates.

4 Hayley with Marnie McBean, triple
   Olympic gold medallist in rowing and
   manager of Olympic preparation for
   the 2010 Games.

5 Hayley and Sidney Crosby, Olympic rookie and hero of the men's gold-medal hockey game.

6 Television star Sandra Oh gets down with the Mounties at Team Canada's welcoming ceremony and flag-raising event.

7 Flag-bearer and speed skating bronze medallist Clara Hughes with cross-country sprinter Chandra Crawford.

6

7

8

10

8   Arnold Schwarzenegger visited the
    athletes' dining hall to offer encour-
    agement to athletes from around
    the world.

9   Hayley and Patrick Chan, the future
    of men's figure skating in Canada.

10 Canada's women's hockey team
    Inukshuk, welcoming fans to the 2010
    Olympic Games (*Hockey Canada*).

11 Hayley keeping in game-day condition.

12 Hayley and Jarome Iginla, who set up
Crosby's gold-medal-game-winning
goal for the men's hockey team.

I also heard rumblings that he was upset they weren't buying into the system, they were getting complacent. It's a dangerous thing. I've been in that movie—in 2002, before the Salt Lake Games, we lost every game to them, and it wasn't for lack of trying. But we came into the big one and we won that gold medal.

It's almost the reverse right now, with the U.S. now on a losing streak to us. Doug Lidster said it best: "We have to remember that until we win that last game, we've got nothing." It's important that we don't get ahead of ourselves. I do know we're going to be the best-prepared team in the world in terms of the schedule leading up to the Games—we will have played about sixty games, most of them tough games that we have had to show up and compete in. The Americans can't match us. We've already played forty games, and they've played just a little over twenty. You may say, "Well, that's too many games," but I don't think so. I'd rather play more games and have the chance to be well prepared and mentally solid.

It was a terrific win and great to win in Canada. The first period was interesting because it was a test of how our young players might react to a pro-Canadian crowd, a big NHL building, and a nationally televised game, which is what we will experience at the Olympics. We were tight and we played tight. We're going to have to deal with that and come out better, imagine ourselves in the same situation with a full capacity arena, on national TV, in an Olympic gold medal final.

DECEMBER 19

We were on the road again this week, to Medicine Hat and Lethbridge, to play more Midget AAA games. We lost 2-1 in Medicine Hat. We played terribly. I don't care if people say, "Oh, you're coming off an emotional high from playing the U.S." It's no excuse.

We can play any time, anywhere, and it shouldn't matter. Even if it's in some barn in Medicine Hat, we should be able to play well. We were bad.

On to Lethbridge. We arrived late but we had to get up for a 9 AM practice and pre-game skate and then an afternoon rest before the game at 8:30 that night. It might have been a day where the coach said, "Hey, we'll just have a little beach run, everybody can chill out." But she chose to have a pre-game skate. The team was obviously exhausted. We got to that game in Lethbridge, against one of the best teams in Alberta, and things went downhill quickly.

I was feeling great in the pre-game warm-up on the ice. I did some evasive moves, took a really sharp cut, and my back went out on the right side. I felt a shearing pain. I had been joking with some kids in the stands, they were pounding the glass and watching the warm-up. I had been smiling at them, and all of a sudden the smile just vanished from my face. Those children, the look in their eyes was: "Oh no, what just happened?"

I was in so much pain I could barely get to the dressing room. Doug Stacey, our trainer, came in and said: What's going on?" I said, "I don't know, I reefed on my back."

I always judge how hurt I am by asking myself, "If this was the gold medal game, could I play?" At that moment I said out loud to Doug and Robin McDonald, our equipment guy, "If this was the gold medal game, guys, there's no way I could play!"

They took off my skates, and I sat in tremendous pain. The girls went out for the game, and I lay in fetal position on the table for two periods. The team doctor gave me a shot of Toradol in my left butt cheek. After the second period she gave me a shot of morphine in my right butt cheek. By the time I was loaded in an SUV—Hockey Canada employees Trina Radcliffe and Amber Lesage were taking me back to Calgary—I was feeling pretty loose but still in a lot of pain, the morphine didn't wholly take it away. When I got home

Mom and Dad, who live close by, helped me get upstairs and into bed. I didn't really sleep that night. I took some Tylenol 3s and was high as a kite. I just lay there, and they waited on me hand and foot.

Meantime, back at the game, I wasn't the only player who was hurt. Cherie Piper and Haley Irwin ended up with light concussions. Tessa Bonhomme went down with a charley horse. The game was dirty and physical. One of the guys said a mean and evil thing to Gillian Apps, and she gave him a two-hander across the head. I don't care if you're male or female, a two-hander from Gillian Apps, who is six feet tall and about 175 pounds, is going to hurt! Coach Mel later told me, "I'm glad you didn't play, because you would have been fighting people, you wouldn't have been very happy."

Syl came over first thing this morning and worked on my back for more than two hours. I was pretty bummed out. I've felt dramatically better as the day progressed, icing my back for twenty minutes every hour on the hour. Kelly Bechard came over and we hung out, because I couldn't even go to the team Christmas party at Tessa Bonhomme and Catherine Ward's house. I just couldn't move very well. So we watched *Hockey Night in Canada*.

Tomas and Noah are away skiing. When you get injured like this you say, "Yeah, it's bad luck." And it was, there wasn't a soul around me, I did a stupid little turn, and boom, my back was gone. Fatigue was a factor, for sure. They ended up with fourteen out of twenty skaters active in that Lethbridge game. Our games are so physical and the travel is so intense. We need the coaching staff to lighten things up once in a while.

DECEMBER 20

We have the final team cuts tonight. Mel sent out an e-mail, and the gist was: Everyone has to be at the rink at 6:30 PM. Come in the back door, we'll wait until everyone is there, and then we'll meet each player individually. Meetings will take one to two minutes per player. We'll tell you if you've made it or not. Then you'll leave out the front concourse of the building. Take all your belongings with you. Do not pin, text, or phone anyone in the half hour from 6:30 to 7, when the meetings are done. And then the team will be made.

My previous experiences with cuts have never been good. I have gone to three Olympic Winter Games, and the day they chose the Olympic team was always the most horrible of days. I have never been cut from an Olympic team or a national team, but it's tough to see others go through it. I know how much work and sacrifice it takes to make a national team.

My only memory of being cut was when I played Midget AAA with the Flames in Calgary. We had gone to a pre-season tournament in Medicine Hat. There were a few more selections that had to be made, a few more decisions, but I had thought I made the team. I thought I had quite a good tournament. When we came home I got off the bus, and the coach called me into the arena, the very same arena—Father David Bauer—that our Olympic team is in right now. He said, "I'm going to have to let you go. I'm sorry, I just can't handle having a girl on the team." And I got cut.

I probably should have made that team and played Midget AAA. I would have been the first girl to do that. I was certainly capable enough, and I had a good camp. As it turned out it was a springboard for me—I went to play senior women's hockey and later joined the women's national team.

I felt excluded all the time as a girl playing with the boys, especially at that moment. It will last with me forever. Mom was furious, she wanted to take it to court because the grounds for the cut were nothing more than the fact I was a girl. But I remember saying to her, "No, we're not going to do it. Someday it's going to come back around, and this guy, this coach, isn't going to last. I have to take the high road" (and as it turned out, that team didn't make the playoffs, they didn't have a very good year, and that coach didn't last). It was a moment I'll never forget because it changed my life and impacted me deeply.

So I know how it feels to be cut. I know what it's like to fight for a job. When I played professional men's hockey in Europe, I had to fight every single day for ice time, for my space, for my right to be there. It hasn't been an issue for me in women's hockey, but growing up as a girl playing with boys I lived with that challenge.

Everybody knows cuts have been looming for a while. It's been weighing. For myself, I think I know I'm on the team, like many players do—you have to be realistic about where you stand. But I look at players like Kellar, Ferrari, Wakefield, those players are potentially on the bubble and fighting. But who really knows? I've had no conversation or input about cuts with the coaching staff. Whoever gets released, it's going to be hard because they've both been a big part of our team. Kellar has two kids and a lot of experience. Ferrari brings a lot to the team on and off the ice. Right now there's excitement that we're getting a Christmas break, and relief we have gotten to this point. Then there's anxiety about the cuts. I am so looking forward to seeing how this team performs once these cuts are finished. Let's just get this team made.

I feel for the coaching staff, for Mel, having to make these decisions but it's part of their job. There's no right or wrong way to make these cuts. This is basically a carbon copy of what happened four years ago before the Games in Torino—we had our Christmas party, and the next day they made the cuts.

Kelly and I talked about that last night. She was cut in 2006 and we remember it so well. We had the team Christmas party then Kelly, Tessa, and I all stumbled into the basement of my house and slept. We woke up and went to the rink for meetings. Kelly went first, I went second. She was cut. She was so upset, and I was upset because she was one of my best friends on the team.

But the team has to move on. It will be tough tonight, but when the team shows up tomorrow there will be a lot of excitement as Hockey Canada announces the team, the media interviews, etc. I'm going to have to do my best to hide my injury and not walk around too much. I just have to put on a brave face because I'm in quite a bit of pain right now.

AFTER ANOTHER THREE HOURS of treatment today at least I was able to go to the mall with my Dad for an hour to grab a couple of presents. I haven't done any Christmas shopping. It's been crazy. No time. No motivation at all to go to a mall. Meantime, I look at Becky Kellar, who not only has everything bought but she has shipped everything already!

When I hear the word "mall" I think of evil things—a mall is a terrible, energy-sucking place for me. I don't enjoy shopping. But I did have to grab a couple of gifts and start getting stuff ready for Christmas. Dad was kind enough to drive me and help me with that.

I've been feeling a lot of stress lately, a lot of emotion. I'm not sleeping. I'm angry I have a back injury. But it also motivates me and gives me perspective. I've got to come back fresh. I've been playing pretty well this year, but I have to play better. I need to shoot the puck. I need to dominate, I need to carry the puck. I need to not worry if I don't pass the puck. Is somebody going to be mad? Sometimes I think about all those silly things. I need to forget trying to keep everybody happy.

It's snowing, a gloomy day. But maybe the sun will be shining tomorrow when a new chapter of our team opens up. I'm fatigued going into this break. I'm injured. I'd like to play better. And I'd like our team to keep winning.

DECEMBER 21

The last twenty-four hours have been dramatic, to say the least.

We showed up at Father Bauer arena at 6:30 last night. I was one of the first to arrive, along with Botterill, Szabados, and MacLeod. The coaching staff had an orange sheet of paper, on it they had written all the numbers of the players, forwards from oldest to youngest and an alphabetical order, I believe, for the D. We had to meet with them in the order on the paper, so I was second, after Jayna Hefford. The meetings lasted just two or three minutes.

My turn. I opened the Hall of Champions door, walked in, and there were the three coaches. I shut the door. Mel shook my hand and said, "Congratulations. You've been selected to the team. Way to go." I said, "Thank you," and shook the assistant coaches' hands. Mel then gave me a paper outlining the team schedule for the next day, a media day to officially announce the Olympic team. We talked about logistical stuff. Then I looked at her and shook my head as if to say, "This was tough, huh?" I could see the tears in her eyes.

I walked out and met Jayna Hefford in the hallway of Father Bauer arena. She also made the team—no surprise, because she is a three-time Olympian and has been a great player for Canada for a long time. She drove me to my car, which was on the other side of the rink, because my back is still quite sore. We exchanged a few words, mostly "Who do you think is going to go?"

I got to my car. Gina Kingsbury came out. She was in tears. I was talking to Caroline Ouellette, and we both looked at each other, thinking, "Oh my God, did Kingsbury just get cut?" She wasn't a player we expected to see go. But then she flashed a little smile, so we weren't sure. We stood there for a few minutes, just talking, before we finally decided we should go over to the car she was sitting in. We knocked on the window, she looked over at us with a big smile and gave us a thumbs-up. So she had made it! We were relieved.

Then I saw Piper and gave her a hug—she wasn't on the team last year for the World Championships, but this time she made it. I told her I was very happy and proud of her, how far she had come. We figured, not knowing anything, that these cuts would come down to Ferrari or Kellar on D, and we figured young Wakefield at forward would be in tough because of her injuries—she broke her hand, separated her shoulder. She just wasn't able to stay healthy this year, and had she been able to do that she would have made a run for this team. But it was a long shot for her. So we kind of knew she would not be there.

But the two D players had gone back and forth all season. Who was better and who was able to compete? I didn't know. You feel horrible for these teammates because you know some of them are going to go and they're great people. I didn't know what to do. I drove to Moose McGuire's, sat in the parking lot and texted Carla MacLeod and a couple of the other girls. I said, "I'm over at Moose's, let me know after everyone's gone through and what happened." I know, we weren't supposed to be calling each other but I wanted to know so bad! It's not a mean thing, it's just out of curiosity as the drama unfolds. Everyone was just waiting.

Carla replied and said Kellar made it, she knew because she was right after Kellar on the D list. When she said that my heart dropped because I knew the cut was Ferrari. I'm so happy for Becky Kellar—this is a thirty-four-year-old woman, older than me, who moved her two young boys and her parents out here to help take care of everything, to go for her Olympic dream. Her husband is back in Burlington, running his own business. I don't think, unless you have children, you could know how exhausting and how demanding it is as a parent to make the commitment to go for the Olympic team. I'm so happy for Kellar. At the same time there's incredible disappointment for Ferrari—a practical joker, a great person who kept things light in the room, made people laugh, always knew the right thing to say.

I'm sure it was very close. My guess is they chose Kellar because they wanted more mobility, she's a better skater, maybe a little better shot. Many of the girls had been saying if they cut Ferrari it would be a huge mistake because we need that lightness, we need that person who's all for the team and happy-go-lucky. I don't disagree, but at the end of the day you have to make decisions about performance on the ice. I know it's going to affect our team. Some of the players may think, "Oh my God, she's gone, our team's going to fall apart." That's absolutely ridiculous and unreasonable. We're going to find a way, like we always do. We're all working toward the gold medal.

Still, it was tough. I waited at Moose's for some of the girls to show up, some that I'd played club hockey with—Sostorics, MacLeod, Kellar. Kellar's Dad drove her there. He was in tears. I gave her a hug, and her Dad, too. Family members do a lot for us players, they bring a huge commitment to this whole process.

We gathered at Moose's. I had one beer with the girls and celebrated, but it was also a down atmosphere. My back was sore, I had to leave. I decided to see Wakefield before she left for home. She's a young player who brought a lot to the team but just had bad luck. She'll be there in four years, there's no question. Her attitude was good. They have offered team alternate status for both Wakefield and Ferrari.

FAST-FORWARD TO TODAY, Monday, December 21. I woke up able to walk like a normal human being, not all crunched over.

I put on some dress clothes and went to the rink. The atmosphere was like a funeral. The coaching staff came in and said, "Congratulations on making the team." Half the players had their heads down and looked like they had been up all night, and they probably had been! They looked bedraggled. I also understood how they felt about the loss of a good friend and teammate like Ferrari.

But I had mixed feelings because we also had seven young first-time Olympians. I wanted them to be excited and to have other players on the team be supportive. I didn't think it was a very good environment, some of our veteran players weren't handling the cut very well. I know they're disappointed, as am I. I'm not as close with Ferrari off the ice but my friend Kelly was cut in 2006, and I remember how devastating it was. But the next day I had to pick up and move on.

We went down to the Sheraton hotel, and Bob Nicholson addressed the team. He said, "We're proud of you, you're right where we want you to be. You've come a long way, and this is a team that's going to win. Yes, you've lost teammates, yes, you should be upset, I wouldn't want it any other way. But this is also a day of celebration. Be happy, move on."

It was a good message. They took us into another room for the press conference. It was good coverage for us, but at the same time many reporters were saying, "Geez, it feels like there are a lot of mixed feelings in here." A lot of our players were upset. They have a right to be upset but I felt we could have tried to be a little more excited in the moment.

We had our official team dinner at Ruth's Chris, a fancy steak house by the Calgary Tower. By then, people were starting to come around. We sat at tables in a square, facing each other, a really good thing. Everybody was able to interact, see each other. I saw a few more smiles, people started to let go.

I made the toast to the team and to the Olympic rookies, "Congratulations, it's an exciting time. I know there are mixed feelings and emotions, and it affects everybody in a different way. But it's important to also celebrate. You Olympic rookies must enjoy Vancouver because four years from now, in Russia, it's not going to be as good as Vancouver in terms of the whole Olympic experience."

We had a good laugh at that. It lightened things up and people were in a better mood but still tired. We had dinner then a lot of the girls took off, we went our separate ways.

When I came home I lay down and just shook my head. We'd been waiting three years to make this Olympic team. Finally, the team is made and still people aren't happy. They're upset and emotional. I feel for players who invest their lives and time and effort. I really feel for them when they are not chosen at the end of the day.

So it wasn't a great, exciting day as everybody might think. There was a lot of sadness and change. But I am excited. When we come back from our Christmas break it's the final chapter, the final push, the last quarter. We will have to lay it all on the line, and we will.

DECEMBER 22

Officially, we are now Team Canada. I really like the group and the dynamic. We have three goaltenders who, on any given day, can play in the Olympic gold medal game. Kim St-Pierre is our longest-serving goalie and has won many big games for Team Canada. She was a major factor in our gold medal win at Salt Lake City, 2002. Charline Labonté got the start and the win in Torino 2006, she has played in the QMJHL and has been a standout with McGill University. Technically she is, perhaps, our strongest goalie. Shannon Szabados ("Szabby") won top goaltender honours in the Alberta Junior Hockey League, playing junior men's hockey. She is new to the national team but has probably experienced more adversity and tough situations because of her stint playing hockey with the guys.

On defence we have a nice mix of young players and veterans. I'm looking to experienced players like Colleen Sostorics to lead the way. "Stubby," as we affectionately call her—she's a "stubble-jumper" from Kennedy, Saskatchewan—is a solid two-way defenceman. She isn't flashy but remains one of our most consistent players and she is a competitor. Mention the word "USA" and her eyes light up! My good friend Carla MacLeod, a standout at the University of Wisconsin, is another veteran defenceman who will be relied upon for her composure and heady play. She has a dry sense of humour, she's a diehard Reba fan. Her strength lies in game thinking and puck movement. Becky Kellar rounds out the veteran defensive core with her stay-at-home defensive ability and physical play.

Meaghan Mikkelson, Catherine Ward, and Tessa Bonhomme are three Olympic rookies who bring a new dimension to our defence. Mikkelson is physically very strong and a great skater who can play both forward and defence. Like Carla, Meaghan played at the University of Wisconsin, and both of them played under Mark Johnson, the current coach of Team USA. They speak highly of Mark and can offer insight on his strategies. Ward, a standout at McGill, has tremendous offensive ability. She can get herself out of trouble and make something out of nothing, she's a very skilled athlete. Sudbury's Bonhomme, a University of Ohio grad, brings a fun-loving personality and gritty style of play. Not big physically, she is tough in the corners, battles hard, and can play forward on the power play.

There is also a good mix of young and old up front. Jennifer Botterill, Jayna Hefford, and myself, along with Kellar, have played in every Olympics since women's hockey debuted in 1998. "Botts" hails from Winnipeg and was a star at Harvard. She brings a solid physical presence, is calm under pressure, and often shines in big games. She also comes from a great sports family. Her mother was an Olympic speed skater, her father is a world-renowned sport psychologist, and her brother played in the NHL. Hefford, or "Heff," has for many years been one of our best and most consistent players. A product of Kingston and a University of Toronto grad, she has great speed and hands around the net. She has scored many big goals for Canada.

Cherie Piper, Caroline Ouellette, Sarah Vaillancourt, Gillian Apps, Meghan Agosta, and Gina Kingsbury make up the next wave of experienced forwards. Piper possesses a ton of natural talent, and her instincts for the game are second to none. She is built like a bull and is tough to handle coming out of the corners. She also has a big job off the ice as she controls the tunes in the dressing room.

Ouellette and Apps are our biggest forwards at 5'10" and 6'0," respectively. "Caro" played at University of Minnesota–Duluth and possesses a great shot and is a true power forward. Soft-spoken off the ice, she is always a presence on it. "Appsy" hails from a big hockey family, as her brother, father, and grandfather all played pro hockey. She played at Dartmouth College and had great success there. She is a strong physical presence. You don't want to have your head down when you play against her!

Vaillancourt excelled at Harvard. She is fierce and determined on the wing. She is strong and quick and reminds me of a little pit bull because she's always going hard.

Agosta, who plays at Mercyhurst College, is one of our most skilled forwards. "Gus" has world-class speed and a knack for breaking a game open. We love to give her a hard time about her hilarious comments and stories off the ice, but she brings a fun, light attitude to the team. Gina Kingsbury, "G," played at St. Lawrence University and hails from Rouyn-Noranda, Quebec. A great skater with smooth hands, Gina is a tenacious two-way forward who is often counted on to kill penalties and check the other team's top players. Quiet and unassuming off the ice, she plays the game with enormous passion and heart.

Our last group of forwards, also Olympic rookies, completes our team: Marie-Philip Poulin, Rebecca Johnston, and Haley Irwin. Poulin ("Poo") is our youngest player, at eighteen. A natural talent, strong, fast, and skilful, she is an example of the good young players coming up within the Canadian system. Johnston ("Johnny") took a year off from Cornell to play for the national team. She has great speed, she competes hard and makes things happen. Irwin ("Irv") hails from Thunder Bay and played at Minnesota–Duluth. She is a great playmaker and exhibits maturity and composure beyond her years. She isn't afraid to get in opponents' faces, trash talk, or play a physical role.

I love this group. We have all the components to be successful. The only question that remains is if we can put it all together when it counts, in February.

The team is set. We are going to the Olympics, an Olympics in Canada. It's a very special time. It's a beautiful, snowy day in Calgary. It's Christmastime, we have some time off, and life's not all that bad.

We're going to win. I just have a feeling we're going to win. And it's going to be a good ride.

DECEMBER 28

Christmas break is over, and it's back to reality. What a crazy day of travel. If I never get on another plane, I will not be disappointed! The Calgary Airport was insane today, the aftermath of a terrorist attempt on a Detroit-bound plane at Christmas. It took two and a half hours just to get through security. They patted us down in a full check through security, there were RCMP officers everywhere.

Our flight left only about an hour late, not bad considering what was going on. But I'm tired from the day, just trying to keep my back moving, trying to keep an even keel amidst the chaos. But here we are in Minnesota, going for the last push in our schedule leading up to the Olympic Games. We play the U.S. here and then meet them in Ottawa on New Year's Day.

For Christmas, Mom gave Tomas *Open*, Andre Agassi's book about his life in tennis. I brought it along with me and I'm about halfway through it. Interesting. He talks about his coach, Brad Gilbert, telling him not to always try to be perfect—instead of trying to hit a winner on every ball, being steady and consistent is enough to win most of the time. Stop thinking about being the best in the world during a match; just remember that at that point you have to be better than one guy—the guy you're playing. He says it takes twenty-one sets to win a Slam: twenty-one sets, seven matches. Take each set; every time you win one, put it in your pocket, one is done. Good, positive thinking.

That's how I feel about myself and the team as we head into the Olympics. We just need to be solid, keep plugging away, not go for perfection, just have every player do her job and be steady. When I get on the ice, I need to not put the pressure on myself, to have to be The One and be The All. Somebody else may have to do it. I might be covered, they might double-team me. Somebody else may have to step up and be The One. That's how we're going to win.

I JUST GOT A TEXT from Syl, who has been working with speed skater Clara Hughes. Today Clara won the 3,000-metre qualifier to go to the Olympics. Great news! Over the years, I've had the opportunity to do some cycling and training with Clara, as I've often seen her at the Oval in Calgary. We have similar philosophies about sport and life. She is probably one of the most driven, focused, and positive people I know.

It's always hard to get back to work after a break, and I certainly needed time off the ice. I really did nothing but lay low at home. Well, the 23rd and 24th I spent at home or running around getting Christmas gifts. In between Syl worked on my back for three or four hours a day.

We had Christmas Eve dinner at my parents' place with my brother and his girlfriend. The next day Danielle and her husband,

Jared, came down for Christmas potluck dinner at Mom and Dad's. I'm a terrible cook. The thought of even attempting to cook a Christmas dinner like my Mom does is just overwhelming. We had the traditional Christmas turkey, all the trimmings.

I felt so rushed this year. I love Christmas, I love the holidays, and I love getting ready, putting up all the lights outside, putting stuff around the house, just getting into the spirit. Christmas was a big thing when we were kids out on the farm in Saskatchewan. But this year I just didn't feel there was any time for that, it just came up on us so quick. I felt fatigued, largely due to my back. I slept a lot. I went to bed at eight-thirty or nine every night, fell dead into sleep. I tried to get as much rest as possible.

I miss being out at the farm. When our family first moved to Calgary I really dreaded being in the city. I felt caged in. I like being outside. With my back being so sore there wasn't much of a chance to enjoy the outdoors at Christmas. But it was great to spend time with Noah. He wanted Lego for Christmas—and he got it, six or seven boxes! We spent a lot of time playing, and I know all about the Mon Calamari and Count Dooku, all the *Star Wars* characters.

We spent a particularly special afternoon together on the ski jump at Canada Olympic Park. After my back improved, I decided to do the stairs that lead up to the top of the highest ski jump, as a conditioning workout. I only did it a few times because my legs lit up, my quads were extremely sore at the end of it! Noah was a little reluctant at first, so he sat at the bottom of the ski jump. It was a beautiful, sunny day. I went up once, came down, went up again. As I was coming down he started to come up—he ran almost all the way up to the top of the ski jump, two hundred and some stairs!

I stood and looked out over Calgary, thinking, "Nearly twenty-two years ago, I sat on those wooden benches at the bottom of the jump and watched the ski jump competition at the 1988 Olympics.

That was my dream as a kid, to be in the Olympics Games!" It was funny that with the Olympics being in Canada some twenty-two years later, I was running up and down the ski jump tower, looking out at where my Olympic dream first started. Here I was, preparing to take the last steps on this road to my fifth Olympic Games, and they're going to be right here in Canada. It was an interesting moment with my nine-year-old son there, thinking it was pretty cool to be so high up and not be intimidated by the height of it all. In a sense it was a metaphor for what we've been going through in this journey to the Olympics.

JANUARY 1, 2010

Happy New Year! Finally it is 2010, the year of the Winter Olympic Games in Vancouver!

Two days ago we played the U.S. in St. Paul, Minnesota, in front of about 6,300 people. We played well and won 2–1. The Americans couldn't match our tempo, our speed, and our fitness. It was a good game, considering most of us hadn't skated in ten to twelve days. I didn't skate at all over Christmas break because of my back.

We fought through, the legs were heavy, the sharpness wasn't there. It was a nice win, but a nothing win. There was no real emotion attached to it.

We thought maybe the Americans would be hungry to come out against us, that they would really want the win. For us to shut them down was just another blow to their collective psyche. It was interesting walking into the arena and seeing them—usually the Americans practise in just sweatpants with shin and elbow pads. At that morning's skate, they were all in regular practice gear. It appears they've changed their tune and tried to step it up a notch, to show they're more serious before a game.

It's not working for them. When you see subtle changes like that in a team, you know that you're in their heads, you're getting to them, you're making them think, playing mind games with them. It was a key victory for us.

After the game we had to be up at 5 AM to get on a flight to Ottawa via Detroit. We arrived in Ottawa, went to the hotel, and had an hour to get changed and ready for New Year's Eve. We all had our own rooms, a nice surprise! I think Mr. Melnyk, the Senators' owner, arranged that. We went over to the Senators game and had a New Year's dinner with players, staff, and their wives and spouses, but only stayed at the game for a period and a half. Jen Botterill and I did an interview with Sportsnet between periods. Then the team took off, back on the bus, to the hotel. Everybody was just gassed, so exhausted.

Today at our pre-game breakfast, Mel said, "It sucks to be you."

I said, "Meaning what?"

My hockey equipment hadn't arrived. Six of us didn't get our gear—it was stuck somewhere in Minnesota. Mel was right, it sucked. We didn't do the pre-game skate. I felt sure we'd have our equipment before the game. Still, there was a bit of anxiety so we called the Bauer guys, who quickly got some gear over to the rink, as well as some of the University of Ottawa women. I called a former teammate of mine, Monica Dupuis, so I knew I was well covered—Monica had skates that I had given her a few years ago. At least I'd be able to wear my old skates even if I didn't have my actual equipment.

Hockey Canada also had people go to our houses in Calgary and put extra skates on cargo flights to get to Ottawa by game time. People were running around like chickens with their heads cut off. In all my years on the national team I've never not had my equipment arrive for a game day.

The equipment arrived about an hour before the game. With great anticipation and excitement, we played the game in front of more than sixteen thousand people, the largest Canadian crowd to ever watch a women's hockey game. Fantastic! We won 3-2 in a shootout. I played fairly well in the second and third periods, but in the first I couldn't do anything at centre. So the coach moved me to the wing and it just seemed to open up, playing with Vaillancourt and Irwin, two players I haven't played with all year. I seemed to get more chances. I got shots off and became more of a threat out there.

But not being able to score has been frustrating in the last few games against the U.S. I know I certainly create space for other players but I also want to contribute. When you're not scoring the tendency is to try harder, but in this case I just have to relax and let things flow. Trust in myself. That's what I need to keep doing, knowing that it's going to pan out when it matters the most. I was slated to go third in the shootout, but I didn't have to shoot because Jayna Hefford scored a beauty, and Natalie Darwitz of the U.S. missed.

We didn't play great. We didn't play awful. We played better as the game went on. We've swept them 6–0 in our series. This is now an interesting turn of the tide. Just as in 2002 we lost every game and then we won the gold in their country, they're in the position to do the same to us.

There's some great drama building in this final run-up to the Olympics. To end the last game of the series with a shootout— the story just keeps getting better. We are ready, we are better prepared. Not that long ago, the U.S. players were saying, "Now we're going to start preparing, now we're going to start getting ready." I kept saying to myself, "There's no way you're going to pull a rabbit out of your hat and just throw this thing together. That's not how it works." Chance favours the prepared. We are prepared.

JANUARY 3

Before I went back to Calgary I spent some time with Bobby Clarke when the Flyers came to town to play the Senators. He always makes me feel so good about the game, my view of the game, and my position. Chatting with him, and guys like Paul Holmgren, guys who have been around the team since I went to their camp in 1998, brings back so many memories

We talked about the pressure of playing. The only pressure you have is your responsibility to your teammates. When you think about the extra pressures, such as having to score because your grandpa's in the stands or because there are seventeen thousand people watching, those things can really take away from your performance. You just have to play. Bobby re-affirmed that with me, reassured me about those things. I can bounce things off him. We can talk about players, elite players in the NHL, and what they do. It really set me at ease that I'm doing the right things.

On the way home to Calgary I was watching Air Canada movies and came across one called *In the Zone*. It was so interesting as it profiled some of the great athletes of our generation: Johann Koss, Cathy Freeman, Sylvie Fréchette, Sergei Bubka, to name a few.

Cathy Freeman talked about winning the 400 metres in Sydney in 2000. She said she couldn't bring herself to think about not winning, because it was literally too much pressure on her. I understand that mindset—when you lose you hate it more than you enjoy a win, because there's just so much pressure.

I was in Sydney, playing on the Canadian women's softball team. I remember sitting in the athletes' village—you could see the Olympic stadium across the way. A bunch of us were watching TV because we couldn't get in. It was a moment in my athletic career that I will never forget. The weight of a nation was on Cathy Freeman! What pressure she must have felt in that stadium—one lone, slight Aboriginal runner for Australia. Everyone expected her to win.

They showed her race on the film. It was interesting to watch her body language, the things she did before the race to calm herself down. It was especially interesting given the situation we are in, the situation I'm in, right now. The Olympics are coming to Canada. Everyone will be watching, and the pressure is on us.

Johann Koss talked about pressure, how you've got to thrive on it or it will destroy you. That's where I am right now, just continually finding a way to thrive as the pressure builds, as the vice tightens.

JANUARY 8

Mail always piles up when I'm on a road trip. One of the things that arrived when I was away was a letter, hand-signed by Al Gore, about the David Suzuki Foundation's Play it Cool initiative. It said, "You make a difference," and it came with a DVD of *An Inconvenient Truth* and a few clothing items. I showed it to Noah. He was impressed. He said, "You know, Mom, it's not every day you get a letter from the former vice-president of the United States of America. And David Suzuki? Now that's pretty cool!"

I thought, "Okay, finally I have something about my career that inspires my son, something that I can show him and share with him." So we watched *An Inconvenient Truth,* and I asked him, "Would you like to meet David Suzuki?" He said, "Oh yeah, that would be so cool, Mom! I know so much about him." And he rattled off a bunch of facts.

Then we talked about inspiration and why it's important. I told him, "You're frustrated when you can't get to the next level of your *Star Wars* Wii game. It's just like Mommy. We play these games, I go on the road, and eventually we get to the gold medal final and we win. I get excited, or happy, or disappointed, just the way you do with your Wii. You're frustrated when you can't make it to the next level. But when you do, you're so happy. It's about progress and just enjoying every little detail along the way."

I think he got it. He looked at me and said, "Yeah, I know what you mean, Mom." That was probably the first time I've made a connection with him about what I do and why it's important. It's essential for your kids to know what you do and why you do it. I think Noah loves to watch me do something I love. I need to make sure I show that I love it. Sometimes it's more stress than it is love. It can't be that way.

So my New Year's resolution is to cut myself some slack and not beat myself up too much. Stop being my worst critic. I can also inspire others.

LAST NIGHT THE TEAM CELEBRATED Ukrainian Christmas. Tessa and Catherine cooked an amazing Ukrainian dinner. They made borscht, perogies, cabbage rolls, chicken, and salads. Everybody brought one little thing, and we all had a nice dinner with friends and spouses and the team. It was good timing for us to get together after a couple of timely wins, just to celebrate where we are so far.

At practice this morning, I went on the ice a half-hour before everyone else and practised shooting and skill work. Szabby came out, and I shot on her. I love going one-on-one with her in practice. She is such a great competitor. Neither of us wants to lose, so it's always a battle. It's intense, but we also have a lot of laughs. I feel most at peace on the ice, when I can do my own thing away from the structured practices.

Our team session lasted only fifty-three minutes, even though an hour and a half had been scheduled. At the forty-seven-minute mark Mel freaked out on us, bag skated us, then told us to get off the ice.

I think she sensed we were tired. So it was a little bit of drama. We'd think something was wrong if this didn't happen at least once during the year. We had a quick player meeting and discussed as a team what we thought about the last two games in Minnesota and Ottawa. We played okay but not good enough. The U.S. could easily have won those games. We talked about getting back to good habits, not being complacent, doing the right things.

Also, Mel changed lines quite a bit in the last couple of games. We talked about being resilient when that happens. No matter what she throws at us, we have to just play and not worry. Yeah, it wasn't our best practice but it wasn't our worst. But we picked the wrong day to push her buttons. She'd already had a few frustrating things going on away from the ice, I think, and that's why it all came to a head. No big deal. Caro, Heff, and I went down to her office later just to chat about a few things and make sure we were on the same page. We left it at that.

Forty-five minutes of putting out fires after practice. Sometimes I wish I could focus on just being a player. But I can't. That's part of being a leader. Leaders have to make tough decisions and do difficult things. We have eight games left in our season, and from there we must find another gear, because the U.S. is doing the same.

JANUARY 17

Less than a month now until the opening ceremonies of the Winter Olympics. My fatigue level is quite high. I'm trying to focus on eating well and getting as much sleep as I can. I slept in until 9:30 AM today. Noah was great—I had told him if he was going to get up early he would have to be very quiet. He woke up before me, and I didn't hear him make a peep. Tomas is out of town again. Noah is playing with his friend Isaac, and I'm on the couch watching TV, doing absolutely nothing, thinking I should probably get up and clean the house, finish the laundry, and do a variety of things. But I'm too lazy.

What I did do today was call the Red Cross to make a donation to Haiti Earthquake Relief on behalf of our team—$1,800 that the girls raised on Friday. What an unbelievably devastating thing!

I'm a news junkie. I've been watching CNN and CBC to see what's happening down there. I'm interested in helping impoverished devloping nations and specifically helping children. That's such important work and a place where no judgment is made. No one expects you to be number one. No one expects anything because they know you're there to help them and they see it as a positive thing. Maybe that's why I'm so drawn to it.

I also talked with Noah about helping his school collect change for Haiti, having kids just bring in their loose change. He's going to take that idea to his school on Monday and try to set up the initiative with the principal. It's important you do what you can. Our team is not rich but we were able to get together $1,800. Every little bit helps. It's important for a sports group—or any organization—to be socially responsible. Mel's cousin had just landed in Haiti and was killed by the earthquake. So this hits home in a lot of ways.

Meanwhile, the husband of a Hockey Canada employee was caught in the explosion in Afghanistan that killed five Canadian soldiers and *Calgary Herald* reporter Michelle Lang. He's in hospital in Edmonton, so Gillian Ferrari visited him and dropped off jerseys and stuff that our team had signed. Our team is really good at taking care of people and caring about what's happening around us. The girls, coaching staff, and management always do the best they can to rally when help is needed. That's just a terrific quality about our group and about Hockey Canada in general. They care.

There is more to being an athlete than scoring goals or winning medals. You have an opportunity to use your status, your celebrity, your passion and excitement as a means of providing aid or encouraging social change. I don't make millions of dollars that I can just give to a cause and make a difference in that way. But I can promote change by expressing how I feel and by being involved in organizations that I believe in, such as Right to Play and Play it Cool. Everyone can make a difference.

It's easy to coast through life, to sit on the fence. There are times when we really need to stand up and say something isn't right, something has to change, we can make a difference. Athletes can do that because people pay attention to us, they listen. So when the earthquake hit in Haiti I felt compelled to get my team to raise some money and raise our consciousness about what's going on in the world. Athletes tend to live in a bubble and become susceptible to the Disease of Me—as an athlete I can get caught up in what I need, what I want in order to feel good. Getting outside of that bubble, being part of something bigger, helps you cope with the pressure and expectation of being in the public eye.

Sport can seem so trivial if it comes down to performance, to winning or losing. At the end of the day, who really cares about those things when people in Haiti are dying in an earthquake? It's important to bring things back into perspective, to what is important in life. At the end of the day it's all about the relationships we have with people and the legacy that we leave.

WE'VE BEEN TOLD OUR PRE-OLYMPIC camp will be in Jasper. We stay there from January 31 to February 5, come back for one day, then travel to the Olympics and the athletes' village. I'm excited about going to Jasper. It's time to get away from here, from life and the stresses of being at home. At the same time, I hate leaving Noah—between the camp and the Games, I'll be away from home for a month. I've done it many times, but it's never easy.

This week we're back on the road again for Midget AAA games in Fort Saskatchewan, Lloydminster, and back to Edmonton one last time. We have five Midget games left before we head to our camp in Jasper. I'm looking forward to it. Our team's in a good spot, but the fatigue factor is quite high. The girls are feeling tapped out.

At times I question our schedule, our practices, and everything that we're putting into it. I consider myself a pretty resilient, fit person, and if I'm feeling this, I can damn well bet the younger players, all the players, are feeling it as well. I think Mel has in mind the general idea of taper—soon we'll have less volume, more intensity, shorter practices, less time at the rink, getting ourselves mentally prepared and ready to go. I just hope she is listening to the people around her—physiologists and the strength and conditioning people. Sometimes, in this environment, you're on an island by yourself and it's hard to trust those around you. But for the most part she does a good job of listening and making adjustments.

Right now our days as a team consist of eating, sleeping, playing hockey, and trying to recover. I'm just trying to keep my head above water.

JANUARY 18

Mark Messier is in town. He's the general manager of the men's national team for the upcoming World Championships this year. John Misley, the vice-president of Hockey Canada, asked if our team would like to meet with Mark, and I said, "Yes, for sure!" But a lot of the girls felt that, having just one day off in a long while, they wanted to rest completely, and they opted out of the evening. So five of us—Caroline Ouellette, Kim St-Pierre, Carla MacLeod, Meaghan Mikkelson, and I—had dinner last night with Mark, his father, and his uncle Victor.

You might think he would be disappointed that only five team members took advantage of the opportunity, but Mark wasn't upset at all. In fact, he understood completely. He knows how important days off are for players, that rest is key. He said if he could impact one, two, or five players, they can help get the message through to the whole team. It was a more comfortable environment for him, and a smaller group probably made for better conversation.

His message to us was simple: don't look to the coaching staff, or anyone else, to give you confidence. He said that when he played and the pressure was greatest, he focused on execution and composure. Confidence has to come from within. Don't look to outside sources for it. He stressed we need to focus on winning but we must also think about losing. He said he always thought about losing so that he would know what it would be like. Whether he lost or whether he won, he was going to handle it.

Wise words. Like Carla MacLeod said, there's a chance we could come home with a silver medal, and we have to be okay with that. We have to be okay with winning, and losing, and think about both things. Therefore, the game at the end of the day isn't about being focused on the outcome as much as on the joy of just doing things for the right reasons.

I find Mark Messier comes at the game from a real spiritual point of view. Hockey can be primitive. You go out there, you work hard, hit people, put the puck in the net, and hope to have success. Sport is so much more than that. It's more about the person, the holistic experience. As an athlete, you can't have success if just one area of your life is in order. Physical, emotional, mental: if you're strong in one area and weak in the others, it's difficult to have success.

I've learned to try to detach who I am as a hockey player from what I'm trying to do on the ice. Yes, we're trying to win an Olympic gold medal. But we want to get to the point where the play isn't for the outcome, we're not playing for winning. We're playing for the joy of the game, beautiful hockey, making great plays, for the essence of what we do every single day. The other stuff just follows. I don't know if I'm there yet but it's a path I have started to wander. I've read a variety of books in the area, such as David Hawkins's *Power vs. Force*. We sometimes try to force things when the real power comes from letting them happen.

Some people vibrate at a higher energy level, they radiate joy and goodness. Others are Energy Suckers, they take the life out of you. The goal is to get to the level where you radiate joy and goodness, that you *are* excellence every single day, you're not forcing something. That's the spirituality of hockey. What Mark talks about is getting everybody to be in a place where they can be themselves, where the joy of the game is there and you're working toward a common goal with no other agenda involved. Then, when you're on the ice and playing, you're able to go to a place where you feel your team can do almost anything. You're not burdened by the expectation of winning or of having success—you're inspired by it.

I want to look at sport and performance out of that lens, rather than thinking I have to be good, I have to be successful. I've tried to change my mindset from I *have* to do this to I *want* to do this. Our coaches have also harped on it all year, that there is a wholeness of a person that has to be there to have complete success as an athlete. Just being the best physically or strongest mentally isn't going to do it. You have to have the whole package. How you feel spiritually changes the chemistry of your body. If your subconscious is free, open, and unburdened, then you're more likely to have success as an athlete.

It was truly an interesting discussion. Mark was also genuinely interested in our team. He and his dad—also a very knowledgeable hockey guy—had some good laughs at how our team operates. They were a little surprised at the schedule we've had: the intensity, the amount of time we're at the rink all day, nine in the morning until five at night some days. Most days. They chuckled about the fact that we're not allowed to wear jeans when we go out as a team, and at some of the regimented stuff, the practice lengths. But it is a different world at the NHL level.

What the night did more than anything was put the girls at ease. It helped me because I try to say many of those same things, but until someone else says it, someone with a little more clout or influence than you have, sometimes it goes in one ear and out the other. To have it come from Mark Messier was tremendous reinforcement.

JANUARY 27

The countdown is on, and everybody's very excited. The most difficult part now is the waiting. We have a couple of games left, then our pre-Olympic camp, and then we head to the Olympics. It's been a great ride. We've played more than fifty games this season, had a lot of fun, a lot of success. Our team is well prepared and ready to go. The best thing is knowing the Games are at home in Canada. I can't wait to walk into the opening ceremonies and hear the roar of that crowd.

Today I was thinking back to the first time women's hockey was in the Olympics. The game has come a long way in twelve years. The evolution of the game, for countries like Slovakia, China, Switzerland to be able to compete, is so important. Russia is also on the horizon, with the Olympics coming there in four years. I hope the Russian Federation invests more in their women's hockey program. I have heard there are a lot of good women players in remote areas of the country but they go undiscovered because the federation doesn't have the money or time to invest in finding or developing them.

There are a lot of good things to look for in women's hockey. There are strong university and college programs in both Canada and the U.S., and there are more players than ever playing in both those countries. In Canada alone there are 85,000 registered female hockey players. For young girls now, to play hockey, to walk into a rink with a hockey bag and a hockey stick, it's a normal, accepted thing in this and many other countries. I would say women's hockey is in good shape. But the strong European hockey nations need to keep improving and investing in their game, right from the federation level down to individual players.

I'm looking forward to seeing the competition in the Olympics, to get a feel for the Games. I'm also looking forward to the world's media paying attention to the women's game. I hope, at some point, we can have some dialogue about professional women's hockey, perhaps a summit series for women's hockey. There are so many possibilities. But in order to do that we need the global hockey community to come together and the best players in the world to play in the same place.

IT'S AN INTERESTING TIME for the team. People are crusty. They're tired. I'm sick. The puck doesn't seem to go in the net for me right now. This past week I played with two different linemates, Kingsbury and Apps. With every game there seems to be a different line combination, which is a challenge.

Right now sickness is translating into frustration and a lot of stress, the stress of dealing with things at home, dealing with the team. There was also some internal—well, not exactly drama, but team stress for me when I planned a snowshoeing day for the team. I wanted it to be a really fun day. But the girls decided they didn't want to do it because they were tired and didn't want to be sore and they didn't have clothes to go to the mountain and blah, blah, blah. It was a sign that the team is tired. But for me it was really draining.

I've decided I need to be like Mario Lemieux: be a presence in the room, don't say a whole lot, but when you do, make it positive. Then go out there and just play hockey. That's my goal from this point forward. Being a captain can be lonely. If I need something, I have to be the one to reach out. I can't just expect people to offer up what I need. I have to be the one to ask for it.

I notice one thing about our team: when we get exhausted we tend to blame and point fingers. I guess that's normal. But that's also a lack of taking responsibility and accountability. We need to get back to that. If our coach is not doing things we like or things aren't exactly how we want, it doesn't matter. We have to play in spite of all that.

Marnie McBean, rower and triple Olympic gold medallist, is going to be manager of Olympic preparation for the Canadian team in Vancouver. She sent an e-mail out to the all the Olympic team athletes. She said, "If you're hating your sport right now, if you're waiting for the Games to begin, then you're probably in the right spot. Basically just trust in yourself, to know that you're good for it no matter what."

She is exactly right. The girls are tapped out. They need a break. But the break is coming. We're heading to Jasper on Sunday for our pre-Olympic camp. We will have one game and one controlled scrimmage there, but we will also have evenings to ourselves, team meetings, some pond hockey time, some sauna time, a lot of R and R time. In general it looks pretty good. I'm just focusing on myself and my own preparation. The team stuff will come.

I met with Ceilidh Price today. She handles my PR and communications schedule. I signed about five hundred items for memorabilia dealers and for our team. I worked out before our practice at 9 AM. Here I am, it's two in the afternoon and I'm on the treadmill again. I pick up Noah from school in an hour. I will take him to swimming and piano. I will get through another day.

JANUARY 31

We are in Jasper. It took us a while to get here. We were supposed to leave the rink at 12:30 PM, but flights with staff coming in from Toronto were delayed. So it was seven and a half hours later when we arrived at the Jasper Park Lodge. We pulled up in the dark, a cranky and crusty group—only to discover a very cool scene that lifted our spirits. The staff and local people were out there with music blaring, wearing Canada jerseys, sporting the "Believe" insignia, banging their sticks on the ground. A full-on game was in progress and hot chocolate was being served. To be in an Olympics in your home country is so special. People exude such excitement and energy.

While we were enjoying the welcome, our equipment manager Robin McDonald and therapist Doug Stacey were taking care of business. We were tired when we arrived but at least we didn't have to travel on the cube van all the way from Calgary. All year long those guys load and unload our bags and set up our dressing room. We just get on the bus and show up at the rink. It's not a glamorous job, unloading bags of sweaty equipment day after day, especially this year with our busy game schedule.

Robin is a true pro. He is meticulous about our dressing room set-up and he likes our gear to be arranged a certain way. We never have to worry about our equipment, Robin rarely misses a thing. I have seen many equipment managers, from the national team to NHL level, and Robin is as good as they come.

It's great to be here. I lucked out. I have my own room with a fireplace and a common meeting area, a king-size bed, and a nice bathroom. It will be a perfect environment for me to wrap my head around the Games.

BUT I NEED TO RECAP EVENTS, particularly from our game on Friday, the 29th. I haven't been feeling well the last couple of weeks, and now I know why. I had to pull the plug in the midst of Friday's game at Father Bauer arena, the last official game in our Midget series. We were playing the AAA Calgary Flames, and the arena was sold out, which was great. Before the game they honoured three women from the military. There were tons of kids in the stands, a lot of people there to cheer us on.

I had a lot of jump but was finding I couldn't catch my breath. Halfway through the game, Mel and Doug asked if I was having trouble breathing. I'd had a head cold and I wasn't feeling good, I knew I was sick and low but tried to play through it. I had to leave ten minutes into the third period because I still couldn't catch my breath. And it was getting worse. My resting heart rate was ninety, and normally it's about fifty.

The doctor looked at me and thought I probably had pneumonia. So away we went to Foothills Hospital! The waiting room was very busy, it probably should have been a couple of hours of waiting, but I was lucky. A woman whose kids go to Noah's school was working there. I also knew the emergency room doctor, who took one look at me and said, "You're not waiting, we'll help you out right away."

They gave me respiratory tests, an ECG, blood work, and a chest X-ray. An average female my age should blow about a 475 in the respiratory test, and I blew about 400. When I'm healthy I should blow well over 475 because I'm probably not an average female in terms of my lung capacity. The test showed that I was compromised. The chest X-ray wasn't super clear, they saw some cloudiness in my lungs, probably some pneumonia had set in. It was kind of comforting to know there was something causing all of this.

So I walked out of emergency at about 12:30 AM. I needed antibiotics and the doc suggested I might have some adrenal fatigue as well, which was no surprise to me. But to get the diagnosis of pneumonia less than three weeks from the Olympic Games—some people might think, "Holy shit, this is the worst thing in the world!" But it was actually a good thing because I had not been feeling right for weeks. It was comforting to know I wasn't crazy, it wasn't just fatigue or a cold dragging me down.

I took the antibiotics and by the next day I felt a huge difference, a huge relief. So I would say it was probably a bacterial pneumonia. I'm lucky I have good people around to help me. I was also lucky to get into emergency so quickly and lucky to get taken care of right away. At times like this you just have to have gratitude, find ways to keep yourself in a positive dimension going into the Games.

JASPER, FROM A TEAM PERSPECTIVE, is just what the doctor ordered. Prior to leaving for Jasper we ended up losing that game to the Flames 5–4 in a shootout. Last Wednesday we beat the Calgary Royals, also 5–4 in a shootout. I don't think the team is playing as well as it did mid-season, but the fatigue level is pretty high. Here, it's a chance for us to taper down, get some rest, rejuvenate. We'll play a couple of games this week, some controlled scrimmage stuff. I like what I see.

Being here in Jasper is comforting, knowing I'm going to get some great rest, some big sleeps. We get to sleep in until 10 AM, practice in the afternoon, similar to our Olympic schedule. I'm looking at our Olympic schedule knowing that it's relatively a piece of cake compared to what we've been through all year. It was amazing to roll up tonight and see the people here in Jasper.

I'm going to do some meditation, write in my journal, decide what to pack for the athletes' village and hang out with my team. When I get home I only have one day to get ready. So here I am, in the Fairmont Jasper Park Lodge, with a Jacuzzi in my own room, loving life even if I do have pneumonia, thinking things couldn't be much worse, or much better!

FEBRUARY 5

We are wrapping up our camp here in Jasper. We have spent the days doing light workouts and fun activities like curling and outdoor hockey. I've finished the meds for my pneumonia, which they determined had probably been lingering for about eight weeks. Today I played my first game back, a controlled scrimmage with the Jasper Midget team. I felt great, scored a couple of goals, I was flying over the ice. I felt I was back to my old self.

The last few days have been kind of a life-changing experience. Jasper is a majestic wonder in the Rocky Mountains. I can walk outside the hotel to a beautiful lake, where kids are playing outdoor hockey, and the mountains provide an awe-inspiring backdrop. Just to have the chance to breathe again, get ten hours of sleep, to not have stresses of real life, has been absolutely wonderful. And rest—deep, deep rest. Wally Kozak gave me the CD of Dr. Wayne Dyer's *The Power of Intention*, and I've spent a lot of time listening to it and taking in all those good messages.

We hit the Games after this respite. Then it's all over. It's crazy how fast it comes and goes. When I go into an event like this I sometimes feel the weight of the world on my shoulders as the captain and a veteran of this team. Lots of things have to happen, and I'm responsible, although more for myself than for what other people do.

Syl wrote me an inspirational message called "Soul Food." She drew a diagram of trying to get to the top of a mountain—a zigzag pattern because it never goes smoothly. On the second page she wrote, "Success—regardless of what's tossed your way, adversity is merely a test of your resolve. Have faith in your abilities and why you were given such gifts. Forge ahead with pride, confidence, and comfort, knowing you're on the right path. You're not leaving anyone behind but rather exemplifying strength and courage. There's no need for worry or fear when you are on the high road. Take positive steps, one at a time, and you will arrive at the top. Persevere, and it's yours. Thanks a bunch for the laughs, and have a super Olympic Games and safe travels."

It was a perfect message at the right time. On top of all this, the people of Jasper have been incredible to us. I leave feeling healthy, rested, excited, and nervous. I also leave knowing I've done everything in my power, and maybe then some, to be prepared for whatever comes my way in Vancouver.

ANOTHER COOL THING HAPPENED to me yesterday. I received a text from Bob Nicholson. All it said was, "I need to talk to you." I thought, "Hmm, that's interesting. He doesn't often text me."

After I replied he wrote back saying, "I need to tell you something at 4 PM." So at four o'clock he got on the phone and sounded a little odd. He said there was someone else on the line—it was John Furlong, the CEO of the Vancouver 2010 Organizing Committee. John said to me, "This is top secret until it actually happens, but we'd like to ask you to speak the oath on behalf of all the athletes of the world at the opening ceremonies for the Olympic Games."

That's a pretty incredible honour! I said, "Of course, I'd be happy and honoured to do it." Traditionally, the athletes' oath is spoken by someone from the host country who is looked upon as a clean athlete and has competed with integrity and fairness, On behalf of all the athletes at the Games, the chosen athlete vows to compete with integrity and respect, without drugs and within the rules of the game in the pure spirit of sport. You're expected to uphold those values and proclaim to the world and your fellow athletes, "This is what the Olympics are about, this is the standard they are holding us to in Vancouver." The officials recite an oath as well.

John also told me it's going to be a very beautiful opening ceremony. My friend, Clara Hughes, was recently given the honour of serving as Canadian team flag-bearer for the ceremonies. And I am thrilled to do the athletes' oath. Life is funny. You can hit a lot of bumps in the road, and then you get some great news like that!

John asked me not to tell a soul, but I felt I needed to tell my parents. They weren't planning to attend the opening ceremonies, neither was Noah or Tomas. I wanted them there so I asked them again if they wanted to come, telling them my secret and insisting they not tell anyone. When I asked Noah if he wanted to go to the opening ceremonies of the Olympics, he said, "Definitely!" I'm also going to bring Danielle because Tomas can't come. She's going to fly in with Noah. Syl's going to be there, my mom and dad and Trina Radcliffe will join them. To have the opportunity to walk in an opening ceremony in my country and be a part of the celebration is incredible. I'm proud of myself and of this honour

I've been given. And I'm so proud of my family. So, six tickets, and $6,500 later, they will be there to see it all, and it will be fantastic.

We had a great team meeting tonight. Mel gave everyone a set of three dog tags. The first one says "Canada—*Lucto et Emergo*": Canada—Struggle and Emerge. The second one was blank. The third had your name, your number, where you're from, and one small word. Mine was "Roar."

We're supposed to dedicate the blank one to someone. I'm going to dedicate it to Noah. I'm going to give it to him before I leave.

It was emotional. We had to go up, pick out a random dog tag, and then speak about the person it belonged to. I picked Lesley Reddon, coordinator of women's high-performance programs for Hockey Canada and a former national team goaltender. I talked about the passion she has for the game and all the things she does for our team, she takes care of the little details that no one else wants to handle. Robin McDonald picked my dog tag. He said I was the most tenacious hockey player he's seen, but that I cared about what people think and I gave of myself.

It was gratifying to hear the good things people said about everybody, and we had some laughs as we looked back on everything we've done to come to this moment. We watched a video about our journey from mile zero at our conditioning camp in Dawson Creek to now, with a thousand miles to go before Vancouver. It was a special evening for all of us. They couldn't have scripted a better ending to this part of our Olympic saga.

I'm proud to be on this team, proud to be representing Canada. I feel the Olympics lift you to another level on the vibrational energy platform, they carry you even when you don't think you can carry yourself. They propel you to heights where you have never been. I've always responded well to the Games atmosphere and I think I will again. I feel like I'm back.

We go back to Calgary at 11 AM tomorrow. One day to pack. I'll go see Noah at his swim meet. And then I leave for the Games.

FEBRUARY 6

Olympic athletes are bombarded by a variety of distractions, things that can wrench attention and focus away from delivering a best performance. Some distractions are minor, perhaps a little thing that annoys you on the way to training, something you didn't like in the athletes' village cafeteria. But these things can add up and mess with your mind and your energy if you're not prepared.

We finished our camp here this morning with a team exercise on distraction control. As a group we created a distraction list, all the things we think we might encounter or might have to handle during the Games. It's quite a list and offers an interesting window into some of the things that can happen at an Olympic Games. I started doing a similar list at our pre-2002 Olympic camp, just as a joke about all the crazy things that can happen. It's become somewhat of a team tradition and something that we all laugh about, although it's serious business to keep distractions at bay.

We'll see after the Olympics if any of these scenarios proved a problem:

1 Security issues; delays getting in and out of the village; long waits.
2 Political demonstrations.
3 Terrorist attack.
4 Injuries or illness to yourself or a team member.
5 Death or injury to a family member.
6 Personal issues.
7 A bad room; a bad bed; a snoring roommate.
8 Lack of personal space; pressure from family and friends to see them even when you need your space, or rest; having family at the Games and *not* being able to see them.
9 E-mails from fans and friends.
10 Last-minute ticket requests by friends or family.

11 Home Games pressure; twenty thousand people screaming for Canada; feeling the weight of Canada on your shoulders.

12 Everywhere you go, people knowing you and cheering for you; more attention than you've ever been used to.

13 Being expected to win; not wanting to let people down.

14 Expectations of sponsors.

15 Other athletes—such as the men's team—in the village, and the distraction caused when high-profile athletes are around.

16 Media attention; TV cameras around the dressing room; more people and increased intensity around the arena.

17 Media who have never seen women's hockey or watch it only every four years; answering the same questions over and over; blowouts in your first two games and media making a big deal out of that.

18 Media looking for dirt to smear us with; a teammate making a mistake with the media that gives opponents bulletin board material.

19 What U.S. players say to the media.

20 Teammates or other people talking only about USA and Canada, even though we're not actually scheduled to play each other unless we make the final; underestimating the other opponents.

21 Famous people making appearances around the team for photo ops, etc.

22 A balance between enjoying the Olympic experience and preparing properly; feeling like you have to take in other events, take pictures and videos of everything.

23 Taking part in the opening ceremonies, then playing the next day.

24 Being drug tested more than once; missing a drug test and being put on the brink of suspension.

25 Teammates not reacting the way you'd like.

26 Coaches and staff not giving you what you need; practices—
   not enough or not the style you want.

27 Bad refereeing.

28 Getting down early in a game.

29 Losing a game, even in the round robin.

30 Equipment—skates, sticks, gloves—breaking, perhaps
   during a game.

31 Dressing rooms not what you expected; soft ice.

32 Fatigue; not enough rest.

33 Not having enough access to massage.

34 Lack of confidence; not feeling ready.

35 Athletes' village food—you don't like it.

36 Weather.

That's our list, quite a list. But each and every one of those
things has the potential to really mess athletes up if they're not
prepared to deal with them.

IT'S 9:30 PM, and we're now back in Calgary. Before we left Jasper,
I decided to take a walk around the lake and I asked Lesley Reddon if I could borrow her goalie skates. I just went out and ripped
around the lake a few times for a peaceful last moment in the
mountains.

Back to reality. On the way home I went to the mall and grabbed
a new iPod and some makeup and picked up a mouthguard from
the dentist. I came home, grabbed Noah, and we had dinner with
my parents.

Then I packed. I got almost all my things into one bag. When
you're an athlete there isn't much to pack for the Olympics because
you get most of what you need when you arrive. We basically just
need underwear and socks and a couple of t-shirts because we're
given team stuff that we're expected to wear, and we have to wear
different things for different events and functions. It's an amazing

package. I actually have a document called "What to Wear at the Olympics." The biggest hang-up about it all is around logos and sponsors. It's quite complicated. We can't wear a Hockey Canada logo, we can't wear Nike outside the rink but in the rink we have to wear Nike—the document is very specific about all that. So the key is not to pack much and wear what they give you. It's kind of like going to a private school—the uniform is the same, we don't have to worry about fashion. So I really like it!

Tonight I wrote Noah a little card, I told him how proud I was of him and how I hoped he was proud of his mom. I gave him the dog tag I received yesterday in Jasper. He thought that was pretty cool. I told him I'd like him to wear it at the Olympics. That was very special to me.

I'm getting excited for tomorrow, to finally get on that plane and land at YVR and see the excitement unfolding around the Games. The important thing is to rest, be prepared for anything and, between the team schedule and games, try and take it all in—you never know whether you'll have a chance to experience another Games.

Marnie McBean sent a two-minute video about the Vancouver Games to all the athletes. I'm feeling positive about the whole thing. I'm at peace. Now it's time to just *be*, to let everything happen. Don't resist or force anything. There's so much going on, just let it come to you. Be a part of the Games and just enjoy it, don't spend too much time worrying about taking a picture of this or that, or trying to control things you can't control. That stuff just eats you up. So I'm looking forward to it. I can't wait to get there and get on the ice again.

It's time for bed. I'll wake up in the morning, take Noah to his swim meet, then jump on the plane and land at the 2010 Winter Olympic Games in Vancouver. Tomorrow, all this hard work will start to pay off. Here we go. I'm ready.

3

BUTTERFLIES FLYING

IN FORMATION

FEBRUARY 7

Well, here we are in the athletes' village! It's 11:50 PM, and sleep isn't coming, despite a full day of travel and activity. It's great to finally be at the Olympics. A tinge of excitement rippled in my stomach as we flew across the mountains and landed in Vancouver.

We were greeted by a group of reporters at the airport. Right away I was surprised to be asked, "So, you had one goal in ten games against the U.S. How do you feel about your play this year?" And I'm thinking, "Are you for real?" When you arrive at the airport you expect to be asked what it's like to be in the Olympics, general questions. This one was the type you'd get at a practice where you can have a discussion and go into some detail. Which number was this on the team distraction list? I have to let that stuff roll off my back.

It's mild—eight degrees and raining. At first glance the village looks like any other athletes' village. We came through security with the bus, got our bags, moved in, and then realized this is by far the best village we've ever seen for Canadian athletes.

We walked into a beautiful penthouse suite that five of us are sharing—two bedrooms and a single. I thought, "Hey, great, I'm going to get my own room, a single." It turns out the single room is like an office space between the two bedrooms. Jen Botterill and Carla MacLeod share a room on one side, Shannon Szabados and Gina Kingsbury on the other. I have a sliding glass door that's paper thin, with curtains for privacy, not even a proper door to shut! Another item on the distraction list.

After the initial shock had passed, I reminded myself not to freak out about it. I went to Marnie McBean and asked if we could come up with a solution. Maybe we could get some foam to put between the doors, maybe some blackout materials for the windows. It's a little disappointing—you'd think you'd have your own door, your own room, but you never know what you're going to get.

And on top of that, Botts and Crib went to try their beds; they sat on them, and they're hard as rock! Like, literally *hard!* There's no way you can sleep on them. Marnie had been joking about us being high-maintenance hockey players so we said, "You try and sleep on one of these." So Marnie jumped on one of the beds and she literally bounced right off it! So then she knew what we were talking about.

In Salt Lake in 2002, I was rooming with Kelly Bechard. One day I was just lying on my bed, reading, and the bed broke in half. No joke, the bed actually caved in, and I was sandwiched in the middle. We were stunned. We couldn't stop laughing. So this certainly wasn't the first, or worst, bed experience I've had at an Olympic Games.

But it's a relief to finally be here in the athletes' village, which is meant to be a home and a haven away from the madness that ensues outside the village walls during an Olympics. Typically the host city just doesn't sleep for two weeks as there are concerts, parties, ceremonies, and all manner of events going on in conjunction with the Games, plus a myriad of people from all over the world who are in town to have a great time. The atmosphere gets even crazier during a Summer Olympics which involves more sports, more athletes, and more people, and is typically held in a very large city.

Right now I'm in a penthouse on the seventh floor of another building with Botts, Crib, and Szabby, who also left their rooms because we just couldn't sleep on those beds. No big deal—we'll get it sorted out, and it won't be a big issue. Otherwise, it feels great to be here after a long day of travel. We're here. Whatever happens, we just have to stay in our own bubble.

My only wish now is for a little sleep. There are windows all around, and the light is driving me crazy because I like my room to be pitch black and very quiet. I'm going to put a towel over my face, pop in some earplugs, and hopefully have a good sleep. I look forward to seeing what the first day brings.

FEBRUARY 8

I slept not too badly. I woke up early, about 7 AM. I met up with Piper and Kingsbury, and we went to the cafeteria. It's actually a tent, a surprising contrast considering the buildings here are multi-million dollar condos. I just thought they might have a nicer dining hall. Regardless, it's totally fine.

They have all the food you could imagine—an Asian station, a halal station, a grill, and a McDonald's, of course, where you can get coffees and smoothies, they have these fantastic smoothies. They even have a statue of Ronald McDonald sitting on a stool. It's an Olympic tradition that the athletes all sign his body. They also have a continental station; they have sushi, things for sandwiches, a panini maker, all sorts of cereals, meats, hot food twenty-four hours a day, which is fantastic. There's lots of fresh fruit, sliced fruit—no berries, though, which is disappointing.

They also have several types of beverages. We have this Coke card on our accreditation that we can swipe to take beverages out of the machines for free—Dasani water, Diet Coke, Powerade, it's all Coca-Cola product.

No Pepsi products are allowed in the village; nothing from McDonald's competitors like Burger King or Taco Bell can come in or out. These companies pay millions of dollars to be official Olympic sponsors so the International Olympic Committee goes to great lengths to protect them.

The food is good. This is only day two, however—I'll see how I feel after twenty days of it. But in general they've done an extremely good job. After breakfast we went for a little walkabout. It was rainy and overcast, but quite warm for this time of year. The village location is beautiful, looking right over False Creek. Across the water is Science World, currently serving as the Sochi Pavilion. We can also see B.C. Place Stadium and GM Place, which for the Games has been renamed Canada Hockey Place, across the water. It is truly a spectacular sight and a magnificent setting for an athletes' village.

An aura of expectation and an enormous energy pervade the village, typical of the atmosphere before the Games begin. People are arriving, finding their accommodation, getting settled, and there is some stress to that because athletes want to get their bearings and feel comfortable as quickly as possible so that they can focus on preparing for competition.

But it is fun to explore the village, and a lot of athletes were doing that today. There are free things that you can gather up inside the village, posters and gifts. These aren't quite like the extravagant gift packages they give to the actors at the Oscars, but there are some useful and interesting items: a beautiful 2010 poster, apparel from various sponsors, pins, bags, coins, and backpacks.

There is also a station set up in the dining hall for athletes to vote for candidates standing for election to the IOC Athletes' Commission, which serves as the voice of athletes within the Olympics. Without athletes there would be no Olympics, so it's important that we have a say in matters regarding the Games, such as doping issues, the Olympic sports program, and input when cities are seeking to play host to the Games. Athletes elected serve an eight-year term, and this year nine candidates are running for two available positions. Canada has two representatives on the commission—sprinter Charmaine Crooks, an Olympic silver medallist, and cross-country skier Beckie Scott, whose bronze medal from the 2002 Olympics was upgraded to gold when the top two finishers in her race were disqualified for doping violations.

We walked around the village plaza, which has a souvenir store. I bought a couple of posters to put up in my room to make it feel more homey. They also have a confectionary where we can get newspapers and general health products, and Visa, another Olympic sponsor, is the only card accepted. The apparel is quite nice, I find, but I'm a little disappointed in the poster selection so far, because I really like to collect Olympic posters. There is also a ticket office in the building, where I picked up my opening ceremonies tickets.

We took a look at the discotheque and casual games area. It has video games, a vitamin water station/bar; Internet, pool tables, Ping-Pong tables, live entertainment every night. It's a really cool set-up, sort of a large Haida hut.

On my way back I ran into an old friend who is working with the RCMP, and her job is to patrol the village via mountain bike. She told me that, as a cop, she was really impressed with the security presence. Even the water is protected. If you jumped into the water here people would be all over you immediately. She said this place is totally locked down and very secure, a very low threat. She also said they're expecting protestors, no question, during the Games. I said, "Things might be quiet now but when people start losing, when people are done their events, you might have some action. Lots of things happen when people, who have had a bit too much to drink, have either won medals or lost medals. As the Games progress things will perk up."

There will also be an exodus, and arrival, of athletes as the Games go on. Athletes who have events that occur at the start of the Games may actually exit the village three or four days after the Games begin. It's bizarre because their Olympic experience is over in what seems a very short period considering all the time and work it takes to get here.

Pretty much every country has its own building, or section of a building, marked by flags on the outside. As I've said, our Canadian building is fantastic. There is a training room, chef de mission office, laundry facilities. It's important to be comfortable, especially for athletes like us hockey players because we play several games throughout the Olympics and spend a longer time here. Everything is set up to help us become part of a bigger team, the Canadian team.

But there is such a mix of cultures within the village! You cross paths with so many people from different nations. And it's not just athletes—there are also dignitaries, sponsors, celebrities, all coming in and out. They're almost like foreign invaders into this Olympic capsule. There is also an unwritten code about life in the village, that this is where people *live*, and there is an incredible level of respect for one another. By 9:30 or 10 PM, the village will be really quiet. Outside the walls there will be immense activity and electricity, but inside it is typically peaceful.

Peace and relaxation are certainly being encouraged within the Canadian quarters—there is a meditation room where we can do yoga or tai chi, have herbal tea, or just relax in front of a fireplace. It feels like a cozy chalet, you wouldn't even know you're in an athletes' village.

The key is to feel as much at home as possible, and for life to be as normal as possible within the village. So I was eager to get my living space organized, like moving into a new house. I had to turn it into my home. I went back to set up my original room. The COC staff was great about exchanging the beds, and Marnie took care of getting some insulation board. I just slid it into the doors to give me some soundproofing. This place is surprisingly noisy and really bright—the blinds are so thin. I'm shocked. Of all the things, the bed and the blinds are probably what I care about most. They can be fixed, it just takes a little willpower and energy. I suppose these are just the general annoyances of settling into the village.

I've put up some posters, some cards I was given, and pictures of my friends and family from growing up in Saskatchewan and of Noah and Tomas, as well as some beautiful scenery pictures.

I also have a neat picture frame that was made by my sister, Jane. It's got Noah and me in the frame and then words all around it: Freedom. Play. Smart. Healthy. Fabulous. Kiss. Discover. Giggle. Strong. Beautiful. Energy. LoveLoveLove. Gutsy. Live. Love Your Life. Happiness. All-Star. Daring. Confident. Dare to Dream. Energy. Live. Love. Unforgettable Dream. These are words she took out of magazines and pasted on to the picture frame. When I look at it I think, "Imagine it, go after it, and achieve it." I will look at that every night before I go to sleep.

I also have a little *Star Wars* character, Amidala, that Noah gave me. She sits here to protect me, as he said. And Shifu, a *Kung Fu Panda* character, and another bear that he gave me to sleep with at night. I also brought a pillow and nice Canada pillowcase made for me by my Mom, and I've bought an Olympic blanket with Olympic mascot Quatchi on it, a nice fuzzy one, and put it on my bed. That's pretty much my room.

AFTER LUNCH WE GOT on the team bus. It took a long time, forty-five minutes, to get to the University of B.C., site of some of the women's hockey games. They say they're already using the special Olympic traffic lanes, but it doesn't seem like they're shut down to general traffic just yet.

When we got off the bus I noticed the volunteers immediately. There were so many of them and they were all excited. Their eagerness to help was almost over the top. Everywhere we turned they'd ask, "Can I carry this for you? Can I do this and that for you?" Doug Lidster told me one woman volunteer came up to him in the cafeteria and told him he was chewing his food too fast! She was just trying to be helpful, and I know all the athletes appreciate the work they do. They're just so keen and excited to have the Games here and they want to do their jobs well, whether it's manning tills or directing lineups. It's weird to be in an Olympics in your home country, because most of the big events we compete in aren't in Canada. Volunteers get on the elevator and I keep expecting to hear accents, only to realize these are Canadians, Canadian people, they live here. They're on our side for a change.

We had no problem finding the rink, there were plenty of volunteers to show us the way! The dressing room looked fantastic. Hanging there was a banner that Noah's school made for us. We also discovered we each had a Nike package in our stalls—runners, warm-up clothes, t-shirts, all sorts of stuff. Everything fit ... sort of. Well, not really. It's too big. We always get stuff that's too big.

Practice time. We took our first steps on the Olympic ice. It was surreal, calm. Nobody was in the rink. I stepped out on the ice and noticed immediately how bright everything was. The boards and bleachers were green and blue and they just popped. It was like, "Whoa, this is the brightest rink I've ever played in." The ice was good and fast, but after a while the puck really started to bounce around. It still needs to be worked in. It will settle down.

As a team we weren't very good in practice. Some people were tired, maybe a little overwhelmed, the session was a bit disjointed. Passes weren't crisp, legs were heavy. I felt really good. It wasn't my sharpest practice, but a good start, skating with Piper and Poulin on the wings. We did a lot of good things. We cooled down and then a round of media interviews took about thirty minutes— CTV, OCOG, Swedish television, the same routine, same old questions. Finally I moved on to the dressing room, did three two-minute VO$_2$ max sprint sets with the team. Some of the girls were picked for drug testing so we had to wait for them. By 4:30 PM we were heading back to the village.

Dinner was certainly good. I had rice, bison meat loaf, and vegetables. From there I raced back to my room, dropped off my stuff, had a massage then went to the Canadian outfitting office to pick up our team apparel.

It was fun to see the enthusiasm in the girls who had never been to a Games before, how excited they were about getting all their goods. I was in and out of there in about fifteen minutes. I tried on my pants—yep, they fit; held the t-shirt up to myself—yep, that looks good; tried on a couple of jackets—yep; made sure the opening ceremonies stuff looked good—yep. Okay, perfect, and I walked out the door.

Meantime, some of the other girls were saying, "You're done, you've already tried that stuff on?" Hey, I've been through the outfitting routine many times. At this point, if the fit is close enough it works for me, whereas some of the girls stayed in there for hours, trying stuff on, getting every little thing taken in. I must say the team clothes are really nice—the opening ceremonies outfit is fantastic. It's stuff we would actually wear after the Games. We've got everything—hats, toques, mitts, boots, shirts, sweatshirts, sweaters, jackets, hoodies, fleeces, you name it. It's fantastic stuff, and we're lucky to get it, a nice package, and a nice bag to put it all in. The first thing you do is put your name on all that stuff. Everyone essentially has the same clothing, and it's tough to sort out if it gets mixed up. So I put my number on it all and hung it up.

It was a beautiful day. The sun was shining, the rain let up after noon. The setting of this village is spectacular. We have everything we need. I couldn't be more grateful to be where I am right now.

FEBRUARY 9

I can open my window and enjoy an amazing view every day here. I look across the village and see the flags of all the countries and the city. The weather is spectacular, a beautiful sunny day. I could just sit and admire the scenery all day, and I did for part of this morning, until it was time for lunch.

The dining hall is always a hub, it's where the action is in an athletes' village. When dignitaries and famous people visit the village they often come through the dining hall. Just after I walked in today Michael Chambers, the president of the Canadian Olympic Committee, came up and asked if I would come and say hello to Governor General Michaëlle Jean. Of course!

She was very kind. I asked her if she was excited to be at the Games, and she said she was, that she was coming to our first game against Slovakia. There we were having small talk for a couple of minutes, with a small army of her security personnel and photographers around us! I put my hand on her shoulder and said, "You know, I think you do a great job for Canada." She softened, smiled, and said, "Well thank you very much." I found her to be very gracious. I've always liked the work that she's done. I think she's a true Canadian, a great Canadian ambassador. I was pleased and excited to meet her. She had about five or six security people around her, quite an entourage.

She came over to our whole team after lunch, and we had our picture taken with her. At the same time Jacques Rogge, the president of the IOC, and his entire IOC panel wandered into the dining hall. He got something to eat and sat in the back of the hall and didn't really talk to too many of the athletes, at least from what I saw. But the IOC is a different ball of wax. They're the kingpins of this show, I suppose. I did see former IOC president Juan Antonio Samaranch and a few of the IOC members also.

You never know who you're going to see in the village. I remember in Sydney in 2000, I was just walking around the village. Nelson Mandela had come in to say hello to the South African athletes. I had a chance to meet him and to talk with him there! What an opportunity. These are just some of the unique perks that come with the Olympics and living in the athletes' village.

TIME TO PRACTICE. We got on our bus and it was another forty-five minutes over to UBC in what were supposed to be rapid travel Olympic lanes. But we had a great session, good tempo for forty-five minutes, much better than yesterday when we were not very sharp. The ice is settling in a bit more, it's not as bouncy as it was. I think the girls were feeling more comfortable today. It's a great venue.

Today there were a lot of people around, not only volunteers but media and just people hanging around. With so many onlookers you end up smiling, nodding, you're constantly saying hi. This is different than other Games because we're at home in Canada—everything is so familiar, and everyone is familiar with us. Many of the Canadian athletes are not unknown faces to these people, they're not just random athletes from some country. People recognize us here. At other Olympics I could go around in relative anonymity, I'd smile and nod but didn't have to engage in conversation after conversation. That's something that will have to be managed here. But overall people are very, very nice and supportive, and that's a boost for us.

We did a workout after practice—weights and core—and bused back to the village. We ate, and then I just went to my room and rested. I sent a few e-mails, talked to a few friends. I'm using my Facebook page to update everyone. It saves me having to talk to twenty-five people. Minimizing the amount of technology I am using is key right now. I can't afford to feel overwhelmed by communications and demands, all the things that are recorded on our distraction list.

There is some advantage to having competed in four previous Olympics. I've learned in advance to anticipate problems or distractions and how to deal with them. The first Olympic experience is always special because, as an athlete, it is something you have worked for and dreamed about for many years. So getting there is in itself a thrill and a dream come true. Competing in the Games can also be overwhelming for a rookie, so while I smile when I see the exhilaration and excitement in some of the young athletes here, including the seven Olympic rookies on our hockey team, I also know the experience can be taxing both physically and emotionally, which can impact performance.

I was nineteen years old when I went to Nagano, an excited, wide-eyed rookie who took pictures of everything, even the door handles in the subway station in Tokyo. I didn't want to miss a moment. I was expected to be an offensive catalyst for our team. I felt incredible pressure. We were not allowed to speak to the media. Our coach, Shannon Miller, thought this would be an effective way to deflect some of the pressure. It turned out to be the opposite, because the media was angry with the policy. It was a good intention but turned out not to be a good idea.

The other thing I remember about being an Olympic rookie is feeling I had to do it all myself. I feel a lot of responsibility here in Vancouver, but this time I understand it's not going to be just me, other people have to do the job as well. But in 1998 we, as a team, collectively choked. In the pre-Olympic period we had won every game against the U.S. and we went into those Games with the pressure of winning. The USA played a lot of mind games, they won a round robin game against us, and it became a heated battle going into the Olympic final. Their team embraced the underdog role and believed. We got really tight, didn't play well, and didn't have the fortitude or ability to come back.

To the day I die, I will never forget standing at the blue line during the medal ceremony. I was almost in denial about losing that gold medal game. I had never imagined not winning. But there I was, standing on the blue line, thinking, "I'm not going to cry, I'm not going to let those Americans see me cry. And I don't ever want to feel this way again." I was completely crushed.

One of the things Mark Messier talked about this year was the importance of seeing ourselves both winning and losing. Going into Nagano, I had never given a thought to losing. I suspect that was the same for many of my teammates. When it happened I didn't know how to deal with failure, and learned a good lesson. In retrospect, that Nagano loss was huge. It motivated me. It changed how I thought about performing, about winning, it taught me to look more at the process than getting caught up in one game, one moment. But at age nineteen, that was one big, tough lesson.

FEBRUARY 10

Not a bad stretch of sleep last night, from about 11 PM to 7 AM. Being right on the water makes for a peaceful atmosphere.

I had breakfast with some team members then went back to my room to rest. Good timing, because just after I left three of our players were randomly selected for drug testing. The drug testers just showed up, nabbed the first three players they saw, and asked for urine samples. It took those girls three hours to go through the process. Two couldn't "go" right away and the other's pH was off so she had to try again.

The girls were really irritated, but that's part of the whole testing program, the ADAMS form we have to fill out. It's extremely detailed. Athletes have to state where they're going to be at almost every moment of the day, with one hour of "whereabouts" testing time that they absolutely have to be at—a specific address—and they have to constantly update this online. For example, if they were to come for me and I wasn't at the place I was supposed to be, it would be deemed a doping infraction. It's very serious.

But not being picked for testing is a good thing because it's a pain in the butt. Don't get me wrong, it's not like I am trying to avoid it or have something to hide. Drug testing is part of the process. I'm glad they do it because it helps ensure the Games are fair and clean. Athletes have to be vigilant about what they eat and drink, about anything they put in their bodies, because the testers can grab them at any time, not just after a competition. When I get a smoothie at the juice bar, I have the option of having some protein powder added to it. I never get that stuff, because I don't know what is actually in it. I constantly have to watch what I eat and drink.

You can't help but celebrate when you're not the one nabbed for testing because it can take a long, long time. Essentially, you have to pee on command, and that's tough for most people. I'm lucky, usually I can produce a sample fairly quickly. I've been tested so many times that it probably takes me only thirty to forty-five minutes, including doing the paperwork. But it's a hassle and an interruption to your schedule for the day.

The drug folks don't care. When they come your way, you have to stop whatever it is you're doing and oblige them. As athletes we are also subject to unannounced tests. The doping people can just arrive on the doorstep at any time. Three summers ago, they arrived to test me—it's hilarious now, but at the time it was not funny. It was my sister's wedding day! I was over at my parents' house, we were getting ready for the wedding. The drug testers showed up at my place, Tomas said I wasn't there but directed them over to Mom and Dad's. They knocked on the door. My sister answered in her wedding gown. I was putting on my bridesmaid's dress, and I had to give a sample.

Fortunately, I was able to "go," which was good—I told them if I wasn't able to "go" they'd just have to come to the wedding with me. They felt bad, and obviously it wasn't an ideal situation. But it just illustrates how testing can happen anytime and anywhere.

And it's an invasive process! You have to pull your pants down, pull your shirt up so that the doping control person can see the urine leave your body. Some testers are more serious than others. It's not a comfortable situation at all. Who wants to be watched when they pee? And it's awkward for the testers because they have to witness it all, and who really wants to watch something like that? Half the time you're trying to pee into a small cup and you end up peeing all over your hand. It isn't very dignified.

There's no room in sport for performance-enhancing drugs, although I understand why some athletes would consider taking drugs. They are desperate to perform and to win. In some cases outstanding athletic performance is their only way out of a very difficult lifestyle or terrible situation in the country they come from. For them, not taking the drugs seems worse than trying not to get caught. So I empathize with why some athletes might be tempted.

But it's completely unacceptable. In women's hockey, we don't see drugs at all. I can't think of one athlete or one country that I would guess is on any form of drug. I don't think drugs help a hockey player. In terms of men's hockey I'm not naive, I think there is use of some over-the-counter drugs, whether they're performance-enhancing or not. We all know about Sudafed. NHL teams play eighty-two games in a season, and it's demanding for players to come up and perform for each game then still be able to relax and sleep afterward, knowing that in the next day or two they have to rev up again for another game. It's no surprise that some players rely on coffee, caffeine, or other things to get up for these games, and then they need something to calm them down at night so they take sleeping pills or use alcohol. Of course, some are also totally clean. But there is this lifestyle that is involved with professional sport, especially a sport like NHL hockey, where you're constantly taking your body up then having to bring it back down in order to be able to go again the next night. I think that's where the dependency or the drug problems lie.

In terms of EPO or human growth hormone or other serious drugs that we've heard about in cross-country skiing or speed skating, I don't think hockey has that problem. Over the counter, perhaps borderline substances—narcotics or alcohol—exist for sure at the NHL level. But I haven't seen them creep into women's hockey. I don't see hockey as being a dirty sport as something like cross-country skiing, which has been plagued with drug issues in the past.

But the temptation is there. It's fuelled by the desperate desire to stay on top or perform to maintain a lifestyle, to escape from unspeakable living conditions, or to cope with expectations that follow success. Everybody wants to be the best. I'd like to believe that most athletes who go to these Olympics are clean.

There is a moral code among athletes. A few years ago, an athlete who trained at the Oval in Calgary tested positive. It was amazing how he was shunned from that particular athlete community, and it took him a long time to build his reputation back up.

Of course, mistakes are made. Athletes can take drugs inadvertently. You have to be so careful about every little thing you take, every thing you eat. One little mistake and your life could change overnight. So when someone tests positive, I try first to offer the benefit of the doubt. But I know there are athletes and doctors and coaches who try to find new ways to cheat the system.

I'm going to win on my own terms, be clean, have success, and feel good about what I achieved. And whatever I achieve, it will have been done through natural or non-illegal methods, by pushing my body to the limit using all the resources available to me in terms of sport science, nutrition, everything I can use that is within legal terms.

AFTER MY REST I hailed a cab outside the village and ventured downtown to pick up some tickets. Life becomes hectic when you travel outside the athletes' village and hit the real world. I discovered getting a cab here, even with my Canada jacket and all, wasn't the easiest thing to do. But I finally caught one at the nearby Starbucks.

Within five or ten minutes of my being downtown, people starting coming up to me saying, "Way to Go! Good Luck! Welcome to Vancouver!" Extremely friendly, extremely happy people. All positive, for the most part, but it took a lot of energy to answer nicely and politely and just deal with the volume of people who wanted to come up and chat. It was a relief to come back to the athletes' village.

That was my morning. I went to eat in the dining hall with a couple of the coaches and staff. With today off, most of the girls were out and about downtown, going to Canada House or different parts of the city, shopping, resting, getting massages. I chose to just recharge my batteries and lay low. The village atmosphere is heating up as more and more athletes arrive. It was a grey, overcast day, but you couldn't miss the brightness of the green, blue, and white VANOC colours absolutely everywhere.

ONE OF THE BIG MOMENTS for an Olympic team member is the official welcoming ceremony for your team in the athletes' village, when they raise your country's flag. They do this for all the teams at the Games and, needless to say, it's a big event. The Canadian team ceremony tonight was no exception.

Sandra Oh, from *Grey's Anatomy*, was the master of ceremonies along with Rick Hansen and former Olympic rower Tricia Smith, vice-president of the Canadian Olympic Committee. The team staff and all the Canadian athletes in the village gathered, and we went to the main plaza wearing our flag-raising ceremony gear. In the plaza was a stage with the beautiful backdrop of False Creek, and there to welcome us all were Prime Minister Stephen Harper, Governor General Michaëlle Jean, VANOC's John Furlong, Dick Pound, B.C. Premier Gordon Campbell, and Vancouver Mayor Gregor Robertson.

They were incredibly excited and very, very proud to be Canadian, as we all were. They welcomed us to the village with a series of speeches and showed us an inspirational video. At one point, Gordon Campbell came up to me, gave me a hug, and said quietly in my ear, "We're expecting you to win!" I had a short chat with Nancy Greene Raine, who talked about how in 1988 in Calgary there was a different feeling because the Canadian athletes weren't expected to do all that well. Here, the expectations are much higher, and Canadian athletes are proud of themselves and each other. I thought that was really telling—we have come a long way as a sports nation. Then they called everyone on stage, there were drummers and dancers, it was great fun. At one point I looked up and there were Botts, Caro, Piper, and Vaillancourt on stage dancing with Sandra Oh.

I had my picture taken with Rick Hansen, Nancy Greene Raine, the prime minister, the mayor, and Michaëlle Jean. I could feel the emotion and the expectations. It was a special night. To look out and see the Canadian flag fly next to the IOC flag is such a special feeling. Every single person there was proud to be Canadian. But at the same time there was an underlying sense, from the dignitaries if you will, that "Hey, we've invested a lot in these Games, you had better do well." As an athlete I was humbled to be a part of the event, grateful to be there and just had a sense of wanting to do well. Amidst feelings of joy and excitement I couldn't help but think, "Oh, here were go, what's going to happen, how will these Games play out?"

I met my police officer friend on the way back to the village and I took her to see our rooms. When we came back down we ran into

Michaëlle Jean and her entourage in the foyer of our village dorm. She was playing ball hockey with some of the athletes! They asked me if I would get in a picture, so I did a photo op with her dropping the ball. I taught her the three taps on the stick and take the ball—it was very cool. She is a joy to talk to, one of the most humble, gracious Canadians that we have ever had in that position.

By 9 PM it was time to go to bed, to get off my feet and elevate them after standing around for a couple of hours at the flag raising. The biggest challenge for all of us here is to learn to stay in the moment, to keep focused and look after ourselves, to avoid getting caught up in the hoopla with celebrities all around. But here we are. The flag is raised. Canada is officially in the village.

MEL HAS TOLD US we're going to play an exhibition game against a Midget AAA team, the Vancouver North West Giants. They won the Mac's Midget tournament in Calgary last year. We're playing them as part of our preparation but it's super top secret—we're leaving the Olympic "clean zone" and going into the "dirty zone," an unsanctioned arena facility, which means taking all our gear to an undisclosed rink somewhere in the city. If anyone finds out, the coaches are going to cancel the game and there will be hell to pay. It's something they want to keep very, very quiet—otherwise, the place would be swarming with reporters and fans, and opposing teams could send scouts. Also, as a non-Olympic site, the rink will lack security. So if the media asks, we're supposed to say we're doing a team activity.

FEBRUARY 11

We played the Vancouver North West Giants today and beat them. Well, we didn't actually beat them because we played this controlled scrimmage thing, which was interesting. They're a pretty good team. On the way back to the village we were supposed to be on our own bus, but it wouldn't start, so we had to get on the Midget team's bus. Crazy, but we made it back, and no one, I think, had a clue where we went or what we were up to!

It was a good exercise because it allowed us to work, under pressure, on our power play and penalty kill as well as last-minute face-off situations. I give our staff a lot of credit for making this happen. No other country is doing this. Yes, there are risks of injury, but we get great benefit from practising these pressure situations.

The team arrived back at the village at about 3 PM, I grabbed a quick bite to eat and then I went to meet Syl at Jenna Hills's house— Jenna works for Lululemon, and her place is about eight hundred metres from the village. We're going to continue meeting there during the Games, it's a quiet place where Syl can tune me so that I'm in top form for the next two weeks.

Next on my agenda was a cab trip to B.C. Place to take part in the rehearsal for tomorrow's opening ceremonies. They took me to the green room when I arrived, but I went out into the stands and shot a couple of pictures of the rehearsal. I got in BIG trouble for that. They told me to me erase them! (I didn't!) Some of the bigwigs—Nelly Furtado, Bryan Adams, Garou—were rehearsing. I got to see who the flag-bearers were, I got to see the whole ceremony from the TV in the green room. I met Jacques Rogge. He was okay, he didn't really have much to say. I always laugh that the Olympics are supposed to be about the athletes, but really it's kind of Pomp and Circumstance when it comes to the opening ceremonies.

But it was neat to be there, to be around Measha Brueggergosman, k.d. lang, and many other famous Canadians. Even now, no one knows yet who the final torchbearer will be. But it's interesting to see behind the scenes, how they pull off one of these things. The dress rehearsals are a big deal. The whiteness of the stadium is almost hypnotizing. It will be an amazing bit of

Canadiana. It's a big, big production when you look at all the work, all the performers, and all the volunteers involved.

Michel Verrault, a short track speed skating referee from Lac-Beauport, Quebec, was chosen to do the officials' oath on behalf of all the judges and officials. So when our turn came he and I went out and we practised twice. I wish they had a teleprompter. I have to look down at a cue card which is totally, totally, totally annoying! Under normal circumstances I would probably memorize it, but I'm just too frazzled right now. I'd rather have the words right there for comfort, in front of three billion people, in case I screw up! We practised, and I couldn't get over how beautiful everything looks, how they've transformed what is essentially a big stadium used for football, concerts, and trade shows into a grand set ready to welcome the world.

The scrimmage and rehearsal made for a long day. It feels good to be back in the athletes' village. I'm tired, and a little bit nervous about reciting the oath. It's a huge honour. It will be neat to walk into the stadium tomorrow night. I wonder what the crowd will be like? I'm sure it will be electric. It's going to be a pretty cool night.

FEBRUARY 12

My hands began to sweat five minutes before I went out to recite the oath. I had tried to stay calm, but I began to think about all the bad things that could happen, like screwing up and saying "Oh, shit" into the microphone, or dropping the cue card, or tripping, or freezing up. As I worked to quell my nerves, the audience observed one minute of silence for the Georgian luger, Nodar Kumaritashvili, who died this morning in an accident in training up at Whistler.

Our team witnessed the tragedy as we practised at Canada Hockey Place. While we were on the ice, the big screen was

showing clips of various events. At one point there it was, his accident. It was terrible. Disturbing. He came down the track with so
much speed, flew off the sled, impact, then his lifeless body just
lay there. Some of the girls happened to look up at that moment,
and we saw him die, right there on the screen. It made me sick to
my stomach. I skated over to Mel and told her they had to find a
way to turn off the screen because the accident kept repeating and
repeating up there, and we just couldn't concentrate.

We went into our lounge after practice, and the trainers were
saying they thought he was actually okay. But I thought, "How
could someone be okay after a crash like that?" By the time we
were ready to leave the building we heard he'd died.

I came back to the village. It was so quiet. On opening ceremonies day the athletes' village is usually teeming with activity and
energy and noise. News about the luge accident had spread quickly.
Everyone was whispering about it in the dining hall. It was a
solemn time, and I couldn't help but think how unfair it was. He
was just a young kid.

Many of the Georgian athletes were crowded around the TV in
the dining hall, just staring in disbelief, in shock, in sadness. The
energetic buzz that usually filled the hall had given way to an air of
grief tinged with respect. Later that day a book was placed in the
dining hall for athletes to sign and convey messages of condolence.
Everyone who came in signed it. But I think a lot of athletes didn't
know how to react. After all, this is an exciting time, an intense
time, yet what happened was so tragic and senseless. Everyone was
trying to find a way to deal with it. People were walking around
in a daze. The Olympic opening ceremonies were just hours away,
with competition beginning the next morning, so there was an
understanding about the need to move on but also a need to mourn
the loss of a fellow athlete.

During our morning practice I had to stave off some of my
own reaction in order to not compromise my performance. I had

to, somehow, let it go completely after seeing it on the big screen. Throughout the day I couldn't help but feel both guilt and anger. I'm here competing, and a twenty-year-old guy on a sled just smashed into a wall and died.

Risk is recognized as part of sport, although there is more risk in some sports than others. As a hockey player, I do think for fleeting moments that I might get hit from behind, become paralyzed, never walk again, or that I could die on the ice. But risk is part of the game, part of what we signed up for when we became athletes, and at this level you're not worrying about life after sport. God forbid that something terrible happens while you're competing, but if it does most athletes would say, "This is where I want to be anyway." If I died on the ice I would want everyone to know that's where I wanted to be, that I accepted the risk, I took the risk.

Life is precious, and unfair. Why him? Why anyone?

I think every athlete felt some measure of conflicting emotion as they took part in the opening ceremonies. I'm sure the spectators had the same feelings, the joy of the ceremonies tempered by unexpected tragedy. So we all tried to find some peace, solace, and respect in that minute of silence.

I TOOK SEVERAL DEEP BREATHS and became enveloped in calm as I stood at the edge of the stage, waiting to go out.

Showtime. It was quite a long walk to get to where we needed to be—probably a good twenty seconds. Michel and I took our time, arrived, and stood on our marks. Everything was white, like a blanket of fresh snow had just settled on everything in the stadium. I stepped forward, grasped the flag, and read the oath as if I was reading it to one giant snowflake:

"In the name of all the competitors, I promise that I will take part in these Olympic Winter Games, respecting and abiding by the rules which govern them, committing ourselves to a sport without doping and without drugs, in the true spirit of sportsmanship, for the glory of sport and the honour of our teams."

There was a bluish light that made the setting so peaceful. I felt the cheer from Canada. I think I had just enough emotion without being over the top. I just read it from my heart, read it the best that I could. Michel read his officials' oath, he was fantastic. We walked off. It is a moment that will be with me forever.

My BlackBerry started buzzing, e-mails were coming from everywhere! It was nice to feel the love from Canada. Tomas said he watched the ceremonies and my oath recitation from the rink of the Canmore sportsplex, and everyone loved it. I wished that he could have been here, but he had to work. It was great that he could see it nonetheless.

We went back to the green room, and I stripped off my jacket, as I was really sweating. I ran into Sarah McLachlan again and talked to her for a few minutes. We ended up sitting beside each other for the end of the opening ceremonies. It's almost surreal—here I am, having stepped on to the world stage to deliver the oath, sitting beside one of my favourite musicians and composers. I could have sat there forever listening to the music go on and on.

There was more drama than even the organizers had planned on when it came time for the lighting of the Olympic flame. They ended up having four people with a torch: Catriona Le May Doan, Steve Nash, Nancy Greene Raine, and Wayne Gretzky. Four huge pillars were supposed to rise up out of the stadium floor, and each torchbearer was supposed to light one of the pillars. Well, there was a glitch! One pillar didn't come up, so Catriona just stood there, clutching her torch. Oh my God! But it didn't matter. It was still spectacular.

Wayne then had to go light the downtown cauldron—fitting, as he is the most celebrated of Canadian icons. But it was crazy. Only in Canada would you see Wayne Gretzky get in the back of a truck in pouring rain. Just hours before they had a huge security contingent to protect the torch from the crowds as the last of the twelve thousand relay torchbearers took it through the city. But now, with the very last torchbearer, Wayne Gretzky, there was no security that you could see, and very few people on the street! He must have been running on the decoy route. Random guys were coming out of bars with beers in their hands, running alongside the truck in the rain and cheering, "Way to Go, Wayne!" It was just so Canadian! We all howled when we saw it.

Poof, it was over. We got on buses and headed back to the athletes' village. We filed through security, and I went up to my room. I was hungry—starving, actually—and tired from being on my legs, even though I had put on some compression socks for the ceremony just to help take the fatigue away.

I called Mom. Noah was having a meltdown—he'd had a long day, and the ceremony was making it a late night. We had planned to meet, but it was pouring rain so we decided to call it a day. I said goodnight and hugs to Noah. I said I hoped he liked the ceremony, and he said, "Aw, it was okay," which told me he was very tired. But the rest of the gang loved it.

What a way to start the Olympics! The death of the Georgian luger tinged the day with sadness, it affected everyone. Reciting the oath was an exciting and nerve-wracking experience for me, complicated somewhat by his death. I wasn't sure how to feel. Here I was, announcing to the world that the athletes here were going to compete fairly. Should I appear sombre? Should I appear happy? Should I wear a black armband? All of this added to the nervousness I felt, but there is no describing the calm that came over me when I went out to recite the oath. A whole mixture of emotions was going through the athletes. There were moments in the ceremony that were full of joy, and everyone wanted to burst with excitement, but the enthusiasm was tempered because of Nodar's death. I felt the organizers addressed the tragedy with sensitivity, class, and grace throughout the ceremony. We couldn't have asked for a better ceremony, they did a terrific job. My favourite moment was when k.d. lang sang "Hallelujah." Man! Wow! She can really belt it out.

End of day and end of ceremonies. It will take me a long time to wind down from it.

FEBRUARY 13

We officially started our Olympics today with a game against Slovakia! This morning people were still buzzing about the opening ceremonies, and many athletes came up to me and said, "Way to go." It's funny, as the athlete reading the oath I had no choice but to succeed. I couldn't fail or stumble or look like an idiot because I'd have to face these people, my fellow athletes, for the next seventeen days! When I came downstairs this morning, hanging in our building was a huge picture of the Canadian team walking into the stadium last night. Very, very cool.

Our team gathered for breakfast in the dining hall, and there was a special visitor—Arnold Schwarzenegger! He was absolutely bombarded by athletes. Apparently he's a good friend of Gordon Campbell and he's been very supportive of the Games. He's a very nice man and he takes time for people. He was great with the athletes. You never know who you're going to see in that dining hall. It's definitely the place to be if you're a stargazer.

Amidst the leftover excitement from the ceremonies there was also a sense of purpose, focus, and jitters amongst the athletes. Competition begins today. Medals will be awarded. For years the athletes here have dedicated their time, their energy, their lives to preparing for these Games. Last night's opening ceremonies marked the end of that one road, that quest to get to the Games, and they were a celebration. It was a chance for all the athletes to really connect with this thing called the Olympics, because once competition begins you're immersed in what you have to do, you're not in tune with what's going on at the Games. You don't see a lot of what's going on because you're absolutely focused on the competition that lies ahead. So the opening ceremonies, for many athletes, are often the highlight of their Games' experience.

Today, it's down to business. Now our team has to perform. There's nowhere to hide at this point: you're either ready or you're not. In a sense the real work is the preparation leading up to this day, raising the bar so high that we don't have to raise it any more at the actual Games, making the Olympics seem easy, if that makes sense.

At eleven o'clock we did a team run around the village and gathered for the last tag of our dog tag ceremonies. Everyone went around the room and dedicated it to someone. There were plenty of tears, dedications to moms, dads, cancer survivors, families, and friends. I dedicated mine to my parents and to Noah, and to the children of the world. I stayed pretty composed, I didn't get emotional. But many of our staff and players got pretty choked up because it takes great sacrifice and support to get to the Olympics, and everyone's story is unique and inspiring in some way. It was a great exercise—great for our perspective heading into our first game.

I rested after the meeting and tried to elevate my legs as much as possible. Then we travelled to Canada Hockey Place. In the dressing room before the game, Heff reminded me to keep with team tradition and honour the Olympic rookies. We gave each of them a pennant with a Team Canada sticker that said, "From Us to You, Welcome to Your First Olympics."

We beat Slovakia 18-0. The crowd was fantastic, totally into it. The building was almost full. The goaltender from Slovakia,

Zuzana Tomčíková, stood on her head, she was huge. She made some great saves. I couldn't frigging score to save my life. I was maybe squeezing the stick a little bit in terms of trying to score. It would have been nice to get a first goal, but I think I ended up with three or four assists. And who cares in a game like that? The girls made it look easy. And we were so excited to be in a building with sixteen thousand people clearly loving our game. They loved the goals, they loved to see Canada do well. The atmosphere was electric.

We had watched Slovakia in practice and we knew they weren't very good. Early in the game we were up 5-0, 6-0, 7-0, despite their goalie playing so well. It's never fun to play in a game where you're winning by that much, or losing by that much. If it was an exhibition game against a club team or the under-22 team we might work on plays or line combinations. But these are the Olympics. You have to go out and play your very best each and every time. So at one point in the game one of our girls said, "Guys, let's do it for Bulgaria!"

Slovakia had to qualify for these Olympics. The world's top six ranked teams, international Group A, qualified automatically for the Olympics. But Slovakia and China made it here after pre-Olympic qualifying events. Bulgaria was one of the teams Slovakia had to beat in their international qualifier, and they hammered them 84-0. So we decided that if they can beat Bulgaria by that much, we can certainly thump them here in the Olympics. We didn't hold back. Athletes go to the Olympics with the intention of putting their best against an opponent's best. Our goal was to show the rest of the world how good women's hockey could be in terms of skills, athleticism, and playmaking, instead of just dumping the puck in and playing a game that was boring for the Canadian fans.

Also, our effort showed Slovakia where they need to go to be the best in the world. We had prepared very hard, obviously, for that first game. We never expected it to be 18–0, but we knew they would be fortunate to score a goal. But that was no excuse for us to hold back.

After the game we did a stick salute to the crowd, and they gave us a standing ovation, then gave another standing ovation to Slovakia. They were especially appreciative of the goaltender, who seemed taken aback by the emotion. The Slovaks are probably used to playing in front of one or two hundred people. To play in front of a huge crowd in a big arena, it was nice to see the reception they received from the fans.

Afterward, the media wasn't too bad. I expected worse. There were the typical questions: Why is women's hockey in the Olympics? Why are there so many blowouts? At the end of a game players have to walk through a media gauntlet, called the mixed zone, where reporters gather and grab them for questions after they come off the ice. That's why Mel did our team wrap-up on the ice. I answered questions for probably a good thirty to forty minutes. It was brutal because I was standing on my skates and just wanted to get to the dressing room. But that's part of the gig here.

I did my interviews, finally got off my skates, and had a little cool down. There was food ready for us when we came back to the dressing room. Awesome! We sat there as a team and watched Jennifer Heil race the moguls. As I watched I thought, "Please God, let her win this gold medal." She finished second, she didn't quite do it. I felt really bad for her, as she was the defending Olympic champion, and there was a lot of pressure on her. I was in Rwanda with her a few years ago and, knowing her personally, I think she was extremely disappointed. It was tough to see. Everyone is looking for that first gold medal for a Canadian on home soil, and we were hoping it would be her.

I don't think there was more pressure on any athlete coming into these Games than there was on Jenn Heil. She was competing on the first day in one of the first finals of the Games, with a great chance to become the first Canadian to win Olympic gold at home. There is so much focus on what that gold medal would mean to Canada. It's everywhere—on the news, in the papers, in the streets, people are talking about who that first Canadian might be. Tomas and I have talked about it, and he said somebody needs to win that gold medal early in the Games because there's too much pressure on the athletes. I agree, I think it's making it hard to just compete. Somebody has to win to take that pressure away.

FEBRUARY 14

It's Valentine's Day, and today Alexandre Bilodeau gave Canada a valentine to remember. He won gold in freestyle skiing's men's moguls!

I had decided to have a quiet day and lie low in the village, just chill out and watch some of the other athletes on TV. It was a good move. In a final run that took less than thirty seconds, Alex made Canadian sport history by becoming the first Canadian athlete to win a gold medal at an Olympic Games held in Canada. The victory was dramatic because the reigning Olympic champion and event leader up to that point was Dale Begg-Smith, who grew up in B.C. but was skiing for Australia. Alex needed a virtually flawless run to topple Begg-Smith, and he did it! I was in our team lounge, and the place erupted when Alex's score flashed to show him in first place. There was one more skier to come down, a French athlete who had the best qualifying score, but he couldn't duplicate his good run in the final so Alexandre Bilodeau was confirmed as Olympic champion. Everyone in the lounge was hugging and thinking, "Finally, someone's got that gold medal, now we can just move on past this and just compete."

His win certainly takes the pressure off the rest of the Canadian athletes. Finally, we get this gold-medal-at-home thing out of the way. Alex is the man, he goes down in history. Great for him! And his family is quite a story. His brother, Frédéric, has cerebral palsy, and in the post-event interviews Alex said his brother was his inspiration. What a family! I choked up a few times. There will be more gold medals before we're done, but no one will forget who won the first one here!

I also watched Clara Hughes, Cindy Klassen, and Kristina Groves compete in the 3,000 metres. Kristina won a bronze medal, while Clara finished fifth, and Cindy was fourteenth. I see them all the time at the Oval in Calgary. I know how hard they work, the sacrifices they make. Yet it's funny how so much of the training and the sacrifice can lead up to a final single run, as it did today for Alex, and he put it all together. So much has to go right, and so much can go wrong, competing at an event like this.

I SENT NOAH AND TOMAS a giant monkey stuffed with chocolate and wished them happy Valentine's. We haven't spent too many Valentine's Days together. It's usually in the middle of hockey season, so it ends up being a long-distance thing. That's probably true for a lot of athletes here at these Games.

Tomas really understands what it's like to go through the Olympic years, what it takes to prepare. It would be nice for both of us not to talk hockey twenty-four hours a day, but that's the reality of our lives. Tomas built his life in Canada around hockey, and our lives crossed through hockey.

His parents divorced when he was very young, so he was forced to fend for himself a lot with his father constantly being on the road. For him to come to Canada and to have such a successful career in hockey is a great feat, as he had to accomplish so much on his own. Our relationship comes from an understanding of what it takes to succeed in the game, the commitment and sacrifice. I respect what he went through, leaving his native country and native language to move to Canada to start a new life. And he respects what I've gone through in hockey, particularly as a girl playing against boys in a male-dominated game.

He has coached women's hockey and he respects it. He believes in the female game. He's worked in the NHL and with the best players in the world, and yet he also believes in women's hockey. That's something rare in the women's game, to have that type of guy with that kind of experience. The game needs more of them. He has worked as a skills coach with the New York Rangers, Florida Panthers, and Montreal Canadiens but probably the job he enjoyed most was serving as coach with the Calgary Oval X-treme women's team. His love for the women's game, and his respect for the game and its players, is extremely high.

Of course, we've had our differences. There were interesting times when I played for the Oval X-treme and he was the coach. He actually benched me at one point. We had a little player-coach disagreement, he benched me, and then we had to come home and try to set all that aside. But for the most part we get along well, particularly when we are exchanging ideas about hockey. Tomas has also helped me, such as facilitating an opportunity for me to train in the Czech Republic with an Elite League professional men's team. We made a summer holiday out of the experience.

We both love Noah. And we are totally okay with the fact that Noah isn't playing hockey. In fact, we are both a bit relieved about it. We just want to see him happy, so we're both guided by what's in the best interest of our son. But we've woven our lives into the game. Tomas has always been my greatest supporter. We're separated a lot through what we do, and I've missed him a lot throughout this Olympic year.

FEBRUARY 15

Game Day. We started off with a team meeting about playing Switzerland, went for a run, and then it was time to eat.

As usual, the dining hall was the place to see and be seen. Girls were going crazy over Alexander Ovechkin and some of the other Russian players in the dining hall. I went over to talk to Steve Yzerman and Kevin Lowe, who were also in the hall, and as I walked back to the table Alexander had his video camera turned on and he was videoing me. This gave me a chuckle because we have a bit of history from Torino. Late in the Russia-Canada game there, Ovechkin ended up in the penalty box, and he saw our whole team was watching. At one point he turned around and gave us the finger. A few weeks later I saw him at a Flames game in Calgary. We talked, because we are both associated with Right to Play, and I gave him a hard time about what he had done in Torino. So we know each other and, seeing each other here in Vancouver, we had a laugh again.

I asked him how things are going. He said, "We just got here, we didn't know what to eat so we had McDonald's." I said, "Yeah, all the Russians are lined up at McDonald's. It's a delicacy." And we just laughed. I asked if he would take a picture with all the girls going gaga over him. They gathered around him, and we got a picture. He was really nice about it.

I also ran into Teemu Selanne, who I know from playing in Finland—we lived near each other over there. And I talked with Valtteri Filppula, who I also know from my days in Finland. He plays for Detroit and is marrying the daughter of a very good friend. I chatted with Jarome Iginla as well. I think the men like being in the village because they are, for the most part, left alone. They don't mind pictures and autographs with some of the athletes, but it's low-key here, especially for the Canadian players. They can be themselves and just hang out. Sidney Crosby, Scott Nieder-mayer, and a few of the guys were up in the athletes' lounge on the twelfth floor, which is open to all the athletes. They just arrived but they're starting to feel right at home, which is good.

I received a cool poster from my old high school, Bishop Carroll. It says, "We Believe in Hayley Wickenheiser—Go Cards Go." My buddy Carla MacLeod also went to that high school, and they sent her the same poster, with the school Cardinals insignia and the Olympic rings. It's pretty big, signed by a couple of hundred kids. Some other cards came floating in. We get mail every day, and I put the cards and posters on my wall to give me inspiration.

We played a pretty uneventful game against Switzerland at UBC. We won 10–1. I got the monkey off my back by finally scoring a goal. I played with Piper and Apps and had a lot of energy. It was a great crowd, lots of energy and excitement even though it was a 10–1 game. The crowd was excited for every goal. But it was hot, literally hot. Ice rinks are normally cold, but with all the TV lights on I couldn't help but sweat up a storm.

Back to the game. There were times I thought our shifts were too long and we got into some bad habits, which we want to avoid. But we had lots of jump, made some things happen, and I really feel we're rolling along. I liked how our line handled everything. The drug testers come in after each game. So far so good, they didn't pick me.

We always have a meal at the rink, which is great. Players can cool down, shower, change then eat instantly to replenish everything they've just spent. If we wait until we come back to the village we've missed a window of opportunity to get necessary nutrition. The set-up has been great so far. There are so many volunteers around the venues. People are calling them the Smurfs because we can't miss them in those blue jackets. They're extremely friendly and helpful, such nice people. We are being taken care of very well.

On the way back from the game, on the bus, we all got Samsung cellphones that get TV. We flipped from speed skater Jeremy Wotherspoon's race in the 500 metres to Alex Bilodeau's medal ceremony, which was awesome. What an inspiring performance. A gold medal can lift a nation, and that's what we're seeing right now. We can really feel it in the city, the energy is heightened. It was thrilling to see him receive his medal. He is such a humble guy, truly a Canadian dude.

In the past, I think Canadians have had a tendency not to celebrate too loudly or too boisterously when one of our own achieves success. But in the last twenty-four hours we have seen the city and the country truly come alive. Alex's victory and this whole experience of hosting the Games have given Canadians good reason to celebrate, and seem to have been a catalyst for an enormous outpouring of emotion and celebration. But I sense a shift here in Vancouver, a feeling of pride and passion that we might have squelched, or at least muted, at other times in our history. The stands and the streets are crowded with people wearing red and white, carrying Canadian flags, and singing "O Canada." We are a people who work hard and play hard. We want to win, and if we do win we have a good old time.

This is just the third day of medal competition. I wonder what will happen next as these Games unfold!

AFTER OUR GAME we drove to Molson Canadian Hockey House and were engulfed in the spirit of celebration. A few thousand people were there and they were going crazy. The big screens had just shown Alex's medal ceremony, and the atmosphere was loud and proud. Everyone was ready to celebrate Ladies' Night. Our team was brought onstage, and we introduced ourselves. The event was emceed by Tyler Stewart of the Barenaked Ladies. Suzie McNeil played a set, then Tom Cochrane took to the stage for a great night of music and fun.

Donald Sutherland was there—he had just come from the figure skating event with his wife, Francine, his son Angus, and his son's girlfriend, Angeline. We've become friends through the Olympic years and have corresponded on occasion. We first met in 2002, when Donald attended the Salt Lake Games and became a fan of our team. His mother had played hockey at the University of Alberta, so he was naturally interested in our game. He was also in Torino in 2006, and since then I've been bugging him to come to our golf tournament in Muskoka, the Ladies First Foundation's Good as Gold Tournament. He hasn't been able to make it, yet, but he's always stayed in touch. Sometimes he sends me random e-mails about what he's doing, where he is in the world. So when I heard he was coming to Vancouver, I asked him to come to our Ladies' Night.

He came up onstage and rocked the house! He was telling jokes, he put on the jersey that we gave him and was going crazy. It was an awesome night to have him there. I said to him, "Don't you ever get tired of taking pictures with people?" He said, "Do you?" And I said, "No, not really." And he said, "Me neither!" And I said, "Yeah, but you're on a whole different level."

He just loves watching the athletes compete. He's very passionate about Canadians and sport, and about our team. He feels a connection to what we're doing because his mother was a women's hockey pioneer. He's a very, very nice man, a true gentleman.

I returned to the village at about 10 PM. People were milling about everywhere, music was playing, fireworks were popping. There's a real nightlife in the city that can be heard clearly in the village. It's a dull thumping sound that comes right into the room. It was a great day to be a Canadian. I love competing. I don't feel pressure at all right now, I just feel excitement and joy. I felt the crowd lifting us, appreciating good plays, good moments in the game. That's what it's been about here in Vancouver so far. It's going to continue to get better and better, and we have to believe that moving forward because the games will get tougher and tougher.

FEBRUARY 16

All in all it was a good day. This morning I went into the dining hall with Szabados and Kingsbury. We ran into Alex Bilodeau.

I couldn't believe how small he is—he's wide but not very tall. He looks so much bigger on TV. (People often tell me I do, too.) We congratulated him on winning Canada's first gold medal of these Games, and he said, "Hey, my gold is just the beginning. You guys are going to do it." All of this has been much more than he expected. He has had so much attention, it's been really crazy for him. But good for him! What a humble guy.

Mel came up with the idea that when a Canadian athlete wins a medal the three captains on our team will write a little note on a card and we'll send it to that athlete. Alex said he got his card and he really appreciated our support. Just talking to him bolsters energy and enthusiasm. Being a part of the Olympics is being part of a bigger team than our own.

We had a hard practice with plenty of skating, a good, solid sixty minutes. We worked on our specialty teams, on low zone, playing in our own end under pressure. We did some full-ice passing in the UBC second arena from 12:45 to 2 PM, and it all worked really well. The team is looking good, the girls are flying. Kingsbury got a bit hurt in practice today—Appsy ran into her and she went down. Hopefully she's okay. Otherwise the team is really healthy.

After practice it was media time again. I did an interview with *Sports Illustrated*. As I've said, doing media after practice is quite exhausting because we have to go directly from the ice to the media zone and then go to the dressing room. We have to stand there in our skates and answer questions. Today, I took the initiative and went directly to the dressing room, took off my equipment, and then went back out to meet the media. Standing around in skates can seriously deaden the legs.

We returned to the village and had a great meal. The food in the village is terrific. There's so much variety. I had a little piece of pizza, a pork chop, some steamed veggies—spinach, sweet potatoes. There are many different types of athletes here, it's interesting to look at them all. You can really tell which ones are the hockey players. Actually, you can pretty much tell any sport by the body type, even walking down the street you can tell if you pass a hockey player, a figure skater. It's amazing how much bigger the hockey players are than all the other athletes. Having said that, the really big boys, the bobsledders, are up at Whistler.

At times, the body type goes hand in hand with the food consumed by the athlete. This is a generalization, but the heavier, more powerful athletes like hockey players tend to eat more protein and carbs and bigger meals. The figure skaters, especially the females, seem to eat a lot more salad. Of course they're still consuming protein and carbs, but the quantities are different. And everyone sticks to the food they're accustomed to eating at a particular time of day. For breakfast the European athletes go for cheese and meat, which is normal in their part of the world, while the North Americans tend to have cereal, fruit, maybe bacon or eggs.

As people get knocked out of competition, or when their events are over, you see them eating less and less of the healthy stuff, the athlete-type food. At that point it's like they're saying, "Well, I've finished my four years of training, my event is done, I'm going to try a high-fat, greasy meal for change."

I MET SYL AT JENNA'S CONDO, and we did a lot of work to get me ready for tomorrow's game against Sweden. It's nice to get away from the village and have a little haven. We enjoy peace and quiet, look out on the beautiful skyline of the city. It's an amazing refuge. Afterward, we walked up to Milestones and had a meal. People there were screaming at the TV because the Canadian men were playing their first game and they won 7–0 against Norway. People were so into it. It's an intensity I've never quite felt at any other Olympics.

I also got a funny e-mail today from Donald Sutherland. After last night he hurt his shoulder and he asked if someone might be able to take a look at it, help him out a little bit. He was hurtin' today. He apologized for dominating on the stage—but he didn't dominate, he was just really funny.

Some of the girls on our team went to the men's hockey game but I decided to sit it out. It's quite a process to go to a game—there are long lines, it's exhausting—and we do play tomorrow at 2:30 PM against Sweden. So after Milestones I just went back and chilled in my room, watching men's figure skating on my little Samsung TV.

Patrick Chan just skated. He finished fifth, had a couple of bobbles, he didn't look great but apparently some of the other men have been bobbling, so let's hope he'll be okay in the longer program. Andy O'Brien is here working with Patrick and he says he has the capacity to perhaps be the best ever. But Patrick has had injuries so they hope he'll be ready.

My parents are still here and they're having a great time. They went to women's curling today. They've been entertaining themselves with the MacLeods and the Kellars. Mom just pinned me and said they are now on the seventeenth floor of the Shaw Tower, and they are having a buffet dinner with Mr. Shaw himself. My father took it upon himself to tell Mr. Shaw how much he liked the phone bundle. Apparently, Mr. Shaw thought that was hilarious. So you never know where you're going to end up at these Games. Family and friends are having a hoot and doing lots of crazy stuff. They're well taken care of and loving every minute of it. I'm not worrying about having to see my parents every day. I know they're totally fine.

A beautiful day, a clear day—it felt like the Spring Olympics, almost the Summer Olympics. Such a fabulous atmosphere. I really, really enjoy being here. I have the passion to play. There is something inside of me that's ignited to go tomorrow, to play great and feed off the crowd. Time to go to bed and do some visualization about shooting the puck.

FEBRUARY 17

Today began much like any other game day. I slept fairly well although I always seem to be awake from 4:30 to 5:30 AM. I must have to pee about nineteen times a night. Maybe I need to cut back on the amount of liquid I'm drinking.

We had a short team meeting about Sweden, discussing what their game plan would be. Then we went for a run around the village. It was such a beautiful morning, ten or fifteen minutes out there, and the body soaks up some vitamin D from the sunlight. From there I had a shower and then lay down for a bit.

I could definitely feel tension. Every game moving forward is a must-win. There are no second chances. We have a sense of urgency, everyone has tightened up. The bus ride to the rink was pretty quiet. During the ride I flipped on Dr. Wayne Dyer's *The Power of Intention*. In one chapter, he talks about your genius, letting your genius flow and not getting in the way of yourself. I listened to that, it was about fifteen minutes long, and I repeated all those good messages and tried to get myself ready. It's the same process at every Olympics. Every game is a matter of convincing yourself that you're ready to go, you're positive, and reinforcing it constantly when bad thoughts come into your head. When one does come into your head, you recognize it, let it go, and move on to something positive. You have to reinforce what's right, be vigilant with yourself, and get your butterflies flying in formation.

We did our typical game warm-up. The Swedes were already warming up in the back of the second arena. They took our spot, which annoyed me. They were playing soccer, blaring their 1980s music, as Sarah Vaillancourt called it, the oldest music she's ever heard. They had a lot of energy, and I thought they'd be fired up for the game.

For us, it was prepare, get ready, as we always do. Some of us play soccer, some ride the bike. I find a quiet space and do my dynamic warm-up, listen to tunes and say good things to myself. As we were doing our pre-game warm-up in the rink I glanced into the crowd a couple of times and couldn't help but laugh. Three guys were dressed up as Puck Bunnies. They were actually wearing bunny suits! I always like to take a few minutes during the warm-up to look at the crowd, absorb the energy that's out there, look into the eyes of some of the kids, throw the odd puck over the glass for them. Just remember why I'm there—for the joy of playing the game. That's good for me, to take away the pressure and remember it's just a game, it's joy, and everybody there wants to see us play with joy.

We came out flying in the first period, and after twenty minutes it was already 5–0 for Canada. Many people, including Bob Nicholson, said our team hadn't played that well in a long time. We completely dominated, and they backed right down, as we have seen them do before. It was unbelievable. The last time we played the Swedes we only beat them 4–2. This game? I don't know what happened to them. They just quit. Everything we threw at the net went in. The goaltender struggled but she also didn't have any help. They just played with no heart.

I'm embarrassed when that happens, but at the same time it's out of our control. We're not going to sit back just because an opponent is awful. We took it to them. The final score was 13–1. Along the way I was able to break Danielle Goyette's Olympic scoring record of sixteen goals, so that was pretty fun. I played with Piper and Apps. We're a good line: we're physical, we make things happen, we set the tone. All the other lines are clicking as well. I thought the tone of our team was one of urgency, of seriousness, we've got a job to do. The Swedes sat back, didn't battle, and we took advantage of it.

I was happy with the game. But I was not happy afterward to have to answer a bazillion questions about why women's hockey shouldn't be in the Olympics. Of course, it's all Canadian media asking, questioning it all. I don't know what they ended up writing but it was probably negative. But I'm not going to apologize. I slammed the Swedes in the post game and said they under-achieved. Apparently their coach, Peter Elander, did the same. They were bad, and we were good.

We had our post-game meal, jumped on the bus, and went to the Hockey House. I saw my parents. Lois and Doug Mitchell were also there. Tom Cochrane and his wife, Kathy, came by. We had a chat. My Dad, who loves Tom's music, was able to get a picture with him, which was pretty cool. He is such a super guy and has supported our team for many years through the Ladies First Hockey Foundation.

I walked back to the village by myself, at about 9 o'clock. I went upstairs to the athletes' lounge. Sidney Crosby and Shea Weber came up and wanted to play Ping-Pong but Meaghan Mikkelson and Rebecca Johnston from our team were already playing. I said, "Come on, guys, the girls will play doubles with you." It was so funny to watch Johnny, one of our youngest players. She was in amazement and so nervous to see these two big NHL stars. I broke the ice and served as referee for a bit. These guys are megastars, they couldn't go anywhere in this town without being swamped. But I think they're very comfortable in the village.

A lot of the speed skaters were up in the lounge. Alex Bilodeau was up there, too. I asked him to sign a poster for Noah, because Noah is doing moguls now. We just chatted about events, laughed, played Ping-Pong, and watched TV. Martin Brodeur and Marc-Andre Fleury were sitting on bean bag chairs watching a hockey game.

The atmosphere was really casual and, probably for those guys, a nice break. They're insulated from the public here. They don't have to interact with fans. Our young players are in awe, for sure, but for the most part they realize these guys are just normal people. In the village they are left alone to do what they need to do. Sid's just a kid, he's a laid-back guy. It was fun to see that and to see the girls interact in the Ping-Pong game with me standing there being the referee.

Not all athletes stay in the village. Some don't particularly enjoy being in the village. They like to come to the Games and have it feel just like normal for them. Clara Hughes is staying in Richmond, close to the Oval. A lot of the speed skaters are opting to do that rather than endure the travel to and from the village.

In Salt Lake City, Catriona Le May Doan stayed in the village but she also had an apartment where she and her husband could just get away from everything. Some athletes prefer to stay with family. In previous Games, some members of the men's hockey team stayed somewhere with their families then came into the village the night before a game. There's no choice for our team, we all have to stay in the village. That was the rule we agreed upon, that no one would stay outside. Nor would anybody want to, in our situation. It's easier for individual athletes. For example, Jenn Heil competed on the opening day of these Olympics and she stayed here in the village for a while, then left, but she will be coming back to it later in the Games.

We do so much in the village as a hockey team. It just wouldn't work to have everyone scattered about. For us, this is a good place to stay, the main rink is close and UBC's not that far away. For me, the village is my preferred place at any Games because being there helps you feel a part of the Olympics. If you're in your own house, you get less of an experience. But for someone like Clara, who has done this so many times, she's fine with being away from it all and she probably needs that space.

After the Ping-Pong game I came back to my room to watch the day's highlights on my TV phone. It's funny, when you're an athlete competing in the Olympics you really don't see much of the Olympics. You're so busy with your schedule that you miss stuff. I like to watch highlights at the end of the day to see what's been happening. The women's downhill was today, and there were some horrific crashes. Anja Pärson of Sweden had a huge tumble right at the end of her run, Georgia Simmerling of Canada crashed. It was a bad day on the slopes. But American Lindsey Vonn won the gold medal.

I phoned Noah and asked him if he watched our game. He said, "No Mom, I watched *Goldmember* on TV." Oh, the perspective of a child! I'm looking forward to seeing him when he gets back here on Sunday.

Onward and upward. We're right where we want to be. Right now I am in my room and I can hear Stephen Colbert across the village near the Russia House. Looking out, I can see maybe fifteen thousand people gathered around listening to him. He's quite a character. The crowd is going nuts.

FEBRUARY 18

Today dawned another glorious day in Vancouver. They are saying it's the warmest winter they've had in a hundred years. Crazy to think I'm going around in shorts and t-shirts at the Winter Olympics. But, despite the sunshine, it's cool enough at night to remind us it's still winter.

The team had a complete day off. Most of us just hung around in the village and rested. I lifted some weights in the morning, some explosive stuff, then relaxed, watched TV. Crib, Kellar, Stubbs, and I watched Christine Nesbitt win a gold medal in speed skating. It brought me to tears to see how hard she worked to get that medal.

And then the men's hockey! Canada versus Switzerland. Man, what a tight game. The Swiss played well, they put us back on our heels. I thought Mike Babcock played too many players—he needed to shorten the bench earlier in the game and give some guys more

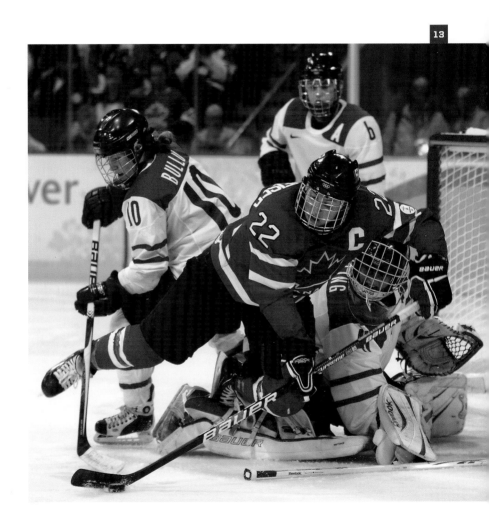

13　Hayley flies to the net in Canada's 10–1
　　win over Switzerland *(Hockey Canada)*.

14 The celebrations begins! Tessa
Bonhomme shows off her gold medal
in the dressing room after the victory
against Team USA.

15 Hayley serves up some golden fries.

16 Ice Dance champion Tessa Virtue and
Hayley out-shine their gold medals.

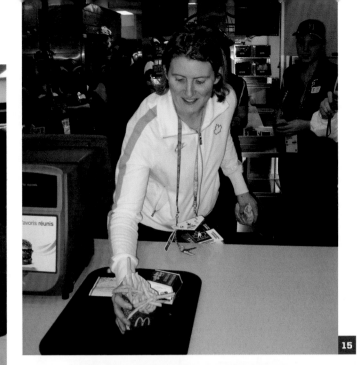

15

16

17

18

17 Hockey player Colleen Sostorics compares biceps with bobsledder Lascelles Brown while waiting for the closing ceremonies to begin.

18 Noah proudly shows off his Mom's new bling.

19 Team Wickenheiser (left to right): Grandpa, Tomas, brother Ross, Hayley, Ross's girlfriend, Amber, sister Jane, father Tom, mother Marilyn, Noah, and Jane's husband, Jay.

20 Hayley's teammate Carla MacLeod
celebrates with skeleton gold-
medallist Jon Montgomery at the
athletes' closing party.

21 Team Canada and well-lit accom-
panists wait in the tunnel to enter
the arena for the closing ceremonies.

22 Captains Canada: NHL veteran and
men's team captain Scott Niedermayer
with women's team captain Hayley
Wickenheiser.

21

22

23

23 "See You in Sochi!" Coach Melody
   Davidson and Hayley reveal their
   plans for 2014, during closing ceremony celebrations.

24 Hayley and Alexandre Bilodeau
   wind down on the final day of
   Olympic competition.

 **24**

ice time. You can't have Jarome Iginla sitting on the bench in the third period. Sidney, in a four-on-four, has to have more than two shifts. It doesn't make any sense. Anyway, for Canada to have to squeak out a 3–2 win was a shock, but coming out of that they will have learned some lessons. They'll be okay.

Good things can come out of a loss or a difficult situation. I look back to our loss in the World Championships last year. Publicly, in the media, Mel questioned herself and her ability to coach our team. We had had a great World Championship, we rolled through the early games, had an excellent team atmosphere, no problems until we got to the final. Then we played Afraid To Lose and we lost the one game, the most important game. The tournament was successful except for that game, and the outcome was that we didn't win the world championship. But the experience provided a valuable lesson for me. Mel questioned not only her leadership but also how I was leading and our team leadership. From that I learned I would have to be much more open with the players, work to communicate better, and have more courage to stand up and call people out when I feel it's not an accountable atmosphere.

Playing on a team can be complicated. Unlike speed skating or luge, where one athlete competes against another or against the clock, success in team sport requires both individual effort and teamwork, it requires communication, cooperation, shared values, and goals. Sometimes you think you're all on the same page, and it turns out you're not.

For instance, last summer at our boot camp in Dawson Creek, we had a race that involved a run, a bike, and a hike. We were divided up into teams, and I was one of the players designated to take on the biking portion for my team. My bike broke down. One of my teammates came up behind me and asked what she could do to help. I was a stronger biker than her. My goal of the whole day was for our team to win this adventure race. So I wanted to do the best thing for the team to achieve that. I said, "I'll take your bike." I grabbed her bike and carried on, because it was about who crossed the finish line first. As it turned out, we won—but I found out later she was crushed that I took her bike, that I didn't believe she was capable of doing the job. That wasn't my intention at all, but that was a crucial in-the-moment mistake for me. I didn't take the time to think of the ramifications of my action, or to listen enough to her, and she was very sensitive about it. And it turned into a bit of a drama that we had to work through.

So you have little moments on teams when those things happen. I'm more of a take-charge, lead-by-example leader, and sometimes I need to just step back and analyze the situation, listen, and find out what's going on. In retrospect, showing I had confidence in her abilities would have done more for our team than finishing first in that particular race. Sometimes it's not about finishing first, it's about bringing the team forward so that you can truly succeed when it's most important. That was a valuable lesson for me that I carried through this Olympic year. It's not about me scoring another goal, it's about making people feel good, let's get this team rolling along, because that's how we're going to win.

FEBRUARY 19

What an emotional night. I was in the athletes' lounge and watched Jon Montgomery win the skeleton. I was up there with Kellar, some of the speed skaters. Sidney Crosby and Shea Weber were playing Ping-Pong, but they came over when Jon came down and we cheered him all the way.

He's an auctioneer who trains in Calgary and comes from Russell, Manitoba. He's one of those athletes who doesn't get a lot of limelight except once every four years when the Olympics come around. I've seen him do auctions to raise money for charity. He's a fun-loving guy, a good auctioneer. And he's a character!

Well, he probably had the run of his life. The elation, the emotion, the satisfaction on his face was so great to see. Then we all had to wait for the Latvian to come down, the last competitor. This may sound a bit unsportsmanlike but we were yelling for him to make a mistake, to do something and screw up. Sure enough, he bumped the wall, and Jon's time remained the best. We all jumped up in the air and screamed. It was really a great moment.

I met Christine Nesbitt as I was coming back to my room. Yesterday she won speed skating gold in the 1,000 metres, one of the gutsiest races I've seen in a long time. She told me, "I totally panicked off the start. I was a favourite, maybe I was in denial about being a favourite and handling the pressure. And it got to me. Instead of just skating from the start I ran off the start. However you start in a sprint race like a 1,000 metres is how you go—if you start slow you go slow, if you start running, you run." She basically ran the whole race. I asked her if she'd been out of synch, and she confirmed that she had been, but had just gutted it out.

I said, "It doesn't matter how you do it, it's the fact that you won—that's the most important thing." She said, "Yeah, you're right. It's the Olympics, man. Sometimes it ain't pretty, but it's how you finish that counts." I was so happy for her and coach Marcel Lacroix, who I've known for a long time at the Oval in Calgary. Just to watch that race, to see her in pain and panicking. She said she wanted it so bad and she went out and got it. It was inspirational, so great to see other athletes doing well.

It's amazing to watch the way people in this country are embracing the Olympics. Stephen Brunt had an essay about Canadian patriotism on TV tonight. People are taking it to a new level—there is a younger generation out there that is proud to be Canadian, has something to say about being Canadian, and wants the world to know. Shani Davis, the American speed skater, talked about how he thinks Americans are patriotic but can't hold a candle to the Canadians. The crowds at the venues have been demonstrating that. The support we've been feeling from across the country has been absolutely amazing. Vancouver is rocking. Everybody's proud to be Canadian.

At the other end of the spectrum, tonight we saw Melissa Hollingsworth, who I know as well from Calgary, finish fifth in the women's skeleton. She was expected to medal. She said she feels as if she let the whole country down. I can empathize with her. I've been there, I know how that feels. In 1998, we were defending world champions yet came away with a silver medal from the Olympics. It's a terrible feeling.

In the course of a few hours we saw the elation of Jon Montgomery and the devastation of Melissa. It's motivating. We just never, ever want to feel the way Melissa was feeling.

BUT BACK TO EARLIER TODAY. We went for another top secret team activity—the official line was we were going on an outing to the Aquarium. In fact, we had another controlled scrimmage against the Vancouver North West Giants at the Burnaby Winter Club. We practised six-on-five situations, power play, penalty kill, some five-on-five stuff. It was useful for us, and we managed to keep the media and pretty much everyone else from finding out about it. The session brought our tempo up and reminded us of things we need to work on in our defensive zone. I tweaked a knee a bit, but I've got some ice on it. It will be just fine.

I also saw Teemu Selanne in the cafeteria. He said, "So you guys play us (the Finnish women's team) in the semifinals on Monday. Oh my God, you're going to kill us!" I said, "Hey, nothing's for certain, games still have to be played." And we had a big laugh about it. We talked about men's hockey and how you can't take anybody lightly. It's good for hockey. Then we talked about our families a little bit. It's great to see all the guys settled and happy here. This village really feels like a home. It's a haven for the athletes, because outside of this place it really is wild.

FEBRUARY 21

What a tragic start to this day! The mother of figure skater Joannie Rochette died suddenly of a heart attack just after arriving in Vancouver. Mel told us the terrible news this morning. When we got to the rink for practice, we stood in the dressing room and had a moment of silence. I don't know Joannie all that well, but what a terrible thing—her mother was only fifty-five years old.

Sometimes life isn't fair, and it's awful for these things to happen at any time. But when they occur on the stage of the Olympic Games, they are magnified even more. I really feel for Joannie. This tragedy puts life in perspective, and it was good for Mel to remind us of that as we stood and paid our respects in silence.

IT'S SUNDAY. THEY CALLED IT Super Sunday here, as there were three big men's hockey games: Sweden versus Finland, Canada versus the U.S., and the Czech Republic versus Russia.

After breakfast I had to do an interview at Russia House for the International Ice Hockey Federation anti-doping campaign. I had to dress incognito to go out in public. By ten o'clock the line was already super long to get inside Russia House. Apparently they have a vodka fountain there. Perhaps I'll get to it when we're all finished. But just being out in the crowds makes me appreciate the safe haven that is the athletes' village—it's comforting to get back to a place where I don't have to be in the public light, not to have to hear what's happening in the media. I don't want to know a lot of details about what's going on outside.

After the interview I met my parents and Jane and her husband, Jay. I don't get to see my sister very often because she lives in Windsor. She's always been a great supporter and more than willing to give me her honest opinion. I visited them for half an hour, came back to the village, had some lunch, and got on the bus at 12:30 PM for our last practice at UBC. It started on a serious note with our silent tribute to Joannie's mom, but then we went out and had a really good practice, a good prep for our semifinal game tomorrow against Finland.

I THINK WE HAVE the best team in this tournament. We have the depth, the speed, the skill, the goaltending—we have everything. We're going to be really hard to beat. We just have to make sure we don't beat ourselves. I keep telling myself, and reminding the others, it's about us.

After the practice we were each presented with a five-thousand-dollar cheque from the Hockey Canada Foundation. Dan O'Neill, the former CEO of Molson, made the presentation. He is retired now and really loves our team, he's been a big supporter for many years. We were told that if we win the gold medal we'll each receive another thousand dollars.

They gave us the cheques while we were in the stands at the rink, watching Finland practice. I'm sure our presence threw Finland off a bit. They play the trap, they will play tough, they'll play with intensity, but they don't have a lot of skill and they are probably better without the puck than they are with it. We need to get to their goaltender early, get traffic in front of her, get the puck up high on her glove side. Then it's all about competing, enjoying the moment, not being tight, making plays we've always made, moving the puck as we always have.

Our practice was forty-five minutes, nice and short. I jumped in the tub, iced my knees, stretched, and took the bus back to the village. I met up with Syl, and Jane and Noah, who had just come back into town with Tomas.

Of course, we watched the Canada-U.S. men's game. How frustrating! I hate watching the USA win. The score was 5-3, and it was the American goaltender, Ryan Miller, who beat us. Brodeur?

Not so good, not so good at all. They'll probably go to Luongo now. What a game, what intensity! It's too bad Canada didn't win but they can still get there. This might be a blessing in disguise.

But what a feeling in the city. There is a vibe that ebbs and flows with the hockey here. People are so into the tournament. Until today the atmosphere has been pretty electric, but the crowds were pretty subdued after today's loss. Sometime after the game, Donald Sutherland called me to tell me how depressed he was about Canada losing that game. Everyone cares in Canada, even Donald Sutherland.

More than anything, I want to go to bed tomorrow night thinking about playing in the final.

FEBRUARY 24

We are on to the gold medal game. One more day, one more sleep.

There isn't much to tell about the Finland game. We beat them 5-0 in the semifinal, and we didn't play particularly well. They frustrate the hell out of you. They play the trap. Their style of play is really annoying. And I didn't think we answered with our best effort. It was a bit of an off game for us.

Our semifinal may have been anticlimactic, but there was still plenty of excitement in and around the Canadian team and, I gather, throughout Canada. While we were scoring our way into Thursday's gold medal game, Canadian ice dancers Tessa Virtue and Scott Moir were winning gold. We missed seeing it live, of course, but there were enough rebroadcasts of the feat to make them a household word in Canada overnight.

I didn't know Tessa or Scott before these Olympics, and I had never met them. But when I heard they had won the gold medal I thought back to an interesting scene I witnessed a few days ago in the laundry room of our Canadian team building. I was with Carla MacLeod and Kimberley Amirault, a sport psychologist, and we had come down to the laundry room because it was a quiet place for us to watch Canada play Switzerland in men's hockey. At the start of the game, a girl came in with her physiotherapist. She said, "Hi, I'm Tessa." Well, throughout the entire game—and it was a long game, two and a half hours—that physio worked on her, from soft tissue work to stretching, not even the smallest detail was overlooked. And the whole session was intense, focused, and serious.

They left as the game ended, and we just looked at each other thinking, "Wow, that was quite the therapy session!" To see the detail and painstaking work that Tessa had to go through to prepare her body—and I'm sure Scott goes through something similar—makes you realize how much effort it takes to compete in figure skating, how precise everything has to be. It's no coincidence they won the gold medal.

And they have captured the Canadian imagination with the win! They're sweet, charming, attractive, and seem to fit together nicely as a couple, although I understand they're not—Scott seems to be more like a big brother to Tessa. But they've known each other since they were kids, so they have this bond that you can see, even away from the ice and when they're walking around. They care very much for each other and understand each other without speaking. Even not knowing them, you pick up on this as an athlete when you see them. Their win was particularly compelling because they were a fairy tale on ice. A beautiful story, so beautiful to watch, and Canadians have wholeheartedly embraced them.

Yesterday was a rest day, so I tried to do just that—rest. The village really is the quietest place in all of Vancouver. It's a safe place. I truly feel like I am away from everything. I haven't read a paper, I don't watch much TV. When women's hockey comes on, I turn it off and go the other way. I'm just trying to stay in a good mindset. I'm continuing to listen to Dr. Wayne Dyer and all his stuff about genius.

I did spend some time with Tomas and Noah yesterday. We just walked around, went to see the Olympic flame, took some pictures. The downtown area is absolutely packed with people, many of them wearing Canadian red and white, but there is also lots of American red, white, and blue; Russia's team gear and the Sochi clothing are popular; you can't miss Sweden's yellow and blue. The souvenir and commemorative clothing businesses must be booming! The streets are crowded, but there is a jovial and cooperative atmosphere, people taking pictures, every once in a while a group will break into an impromptu rendition of "O Canada." I love the energy and enthusiasm. I'm also proud that sport can inspire such a peaceful gathering of people from all over the world.

I have heard some people here rented their houses for quite a bit of money to people from out of town, opting not to stay in Vancouver for these Games. Who would want to miss out on this tremendous experience? I suspect some of them now wish they'd stayed home and taken in these Olympics.

Later in the day I came back to the village and watched what was left of the Canada-Germany men's game. Canada beat Germany 8–2. I had an early night. Nothing exciting.

I HAVE TO ADMIT I'm nervous, a little emotional. Today I met Tomas and Noah for coffee, and then there was a team meeting, which we interrupted to watch Clara Hughes skate in the 5,000 metres. What an exceptional performance. She won a bronze medal—the only athlete in the world to earn multiple medals in both Summer and Winter Olympics. She is an amazing person, a great friend. I couldn't be happier for her. She raced five seconds faster than she did four years ago in Torino, and basically was beaten by a better skater today. But five seconds faster—that was her own personal gold medal. Syl has been working with her, so I know a lot about the work she has put into these Games, and what she did today was a great accomplishment. The girls were all watching the race, and I sat there trying to be stoic, but I got pretty emotional with it all. It was an incredible race.

It's been a remarkable twenty-four hours for Canadian women athletes. Kaillie Humphries and Heather Moyse took gold in the bobsleigh, with teammates Helen Upperton and Shelley-Ann Brown right behind for the silver. Yesterday Ashleigh McIvor won gold in the ski cross, the short track speed skaters earned a silver in the relay, and there's Clara with her very special bronze medal today to cap an amazing career.

And amidst all that, the men's hockey team played Russia today in the quarter-final. We had a late practice, 4:15 PM, which was inconvenient because the men's game started at 4:30 PM. We had to get on a bus and drive twenty minutes to Britannia arena. Throughout the practice our support staff was giving us score updates via hand signals from the bench: 1–0, 2–0, and so on.

As it turned out, Canada just dominated the Russians. They took the puck, they wanted the puck. They took Ovechkin right out of the game, which was fantastic. It was a total team performance, and they won 7–3 to advance to the semifinals. Just looking at the guys in the village this morning, you could tell they were ready to go, there would be no messing around. They all had their game faces on.

Our practice was short, forty minutes, really light, and we had some fun. We had a team meeting. Peter Jensen talked about playing free with an unburdened heart, just go and put it all on the line and skate. Make things happen. Want the puck.

That's what it's going to come down to—winning battles, races to the puck, wanting to be out there when the pressure is the greatest, making great plays, shooting the puck. I'm going to have to shoot, I'm going to have to drive the puck to the net, I'm going to have to be flying. I'm going to have to play the game of my life, as are all the other girls. If we play really well, we're going to win.

We've been told Szabados is getting the start for us tomorrow. She's the right person for the job. She's going to do great. It's going to be a fabulous atmosphere, eighteen thousand people going crazy. I can't wait to get there and play the game, to have a chance to win in Canada.

What would that feel like? I don't even think I can describe it. I'm looking forward to it. I think everybody is. We're in an exciting spot. It's just time to go. There's nothing left to be said. It's been a great atmosphere here—I've lived a relatively low-key and boring lifestyle in the village since I've arrived. But we've had a job to do. At about 7 PM tomorrow, our job is going to be over and we can let loose and do whatever we want. Until then, it's just one more day. Just hang on. Get the job done.

I'm going to smile. I'm going to enjoy it. We're going to be flying tomorrow with the crowd behind us.

FEBRUARY 25

Morning. Gold medal game day. I was a bit nervous when I woke up today, my stomach was doing flips and turns, but I think a lot of the girls had that feeling.

I had breakfast at about 8:30 AM and went for a beach run with the team. That isn't necessarily a run on the beach—it's really just a time to get loose and warm. The term started at a training camp we had in Prince Edward Island a few years ago, where we'd run on the beach every day. Since then it's been called a beach run whether or not we actually do it on a beach. A lot of the girls played soccer in the village. I'm not a big soccer player because of my knees, so I usually just go for a run.

I jogged around the village then did some stretching as I watched the others play soccer. Mark Johnson, the coach of the

American team, happened to walk by and saw the girls playing soccer, me stretching. He came around the corner, looked once, looked twice. It was an interesting moment. I don't know what the American team did to prepare in the morning, or if they even did anything. But looking at him as he looked at us, I imagined him thinking, "These girls are prepared. This team is for real."

This is when things start to ramp up. On the day of the gold medal game I always want to have a story in my head about how it's going to go; what's going to happen; stop any negative thoughts; reverse them instead to the positive. So that's what I did. I kept telling myself all the good things I wanted to do.

We had a team meeting later in the morning. Doug talked about our penalty killing, and Peter spoke about the power play. Steve Yzerman came in and talked to us about preparation, how everything we've done has prepared us for this moment, that we should just enjoy it now. Five or six hours before a game, all we can do is relax. We just need to stay cool, no matter what, under pressure. Don't expend too much energy in the warm-up, just let the crowd bring us up. The girls felt that was pretty cool, we took it to heart. But it's funny he said that to us, because last night I had a conversation with Bonhomme and MacLeod about how Stevie Y always says to conserve your energy and let the crowd bring you up in big games. It was great of Mel to bring him in to talk to us, even just for five minutes.

THE VILLAGE IS JUST MINUTES AWAY, but it was a long bus ride over to the rink. It seemed we were never going to get there. It was a grey and rainy day.

When we arrived there were tons of people in the hallway because Finland was playing Sweden for the bronze medal. They were tied 2–2. We were really cheering for Finland, and they managed to win 3–2 in overtime. They pulled it out. It was an ugly game, apparently. But they won the bronze medal for their country, a significant accomplishment because the three previous Games have featured three different teams getting the bronze medal. In 1998 it was Finland behind the U.S and Canada; in 2002 it was Sweden, with Canada taking gold and the U.S. silver; and four years ago the Americans took the bronze, and Canada defeated Sweden for the gold medal.

We felt relaxed and a bit jittery at the same time. In my mind I was saying, "Stay calm. Keep your energy for when you need it the most, the sixty-minute game." I had been more nervous earlier in the day. By the time I got to the rink, I had calmed down, and those nerves were replaced by a sense of purpose: This is what we have to do. It's finally here. At last I can stop thinking about it.

There were too many people around. I needed a place to escape. I asked if I could go in the men's dressing room and just have some peace. I went in there, watched a bit of TV, talked to the trainers. I went to Sidney Crosby's stall. His stick was there. I looked at it, compared the curve to my stick's curve. It's actually a very similar stick. I just had to take a few breaths, feel the peace and the calm, and then I started my off-ice preparation.

Time for our pre-game warm-up. We walked out of our dressing room, and who was lining the hallway but the American men's team and their coaching staff! They did a little posturing, there was a little arrogance. Later, some of the girls said the guys were chirping, comments like "Hey number 18, your shoelace is untied." The American women followed and, of course, the men gave them a big round of applause. I thought, "Man, that's the kiss of death. You start doing stuff like that, and you're setting yourself up for a disaster."

We went out on the ice, and the crowd was into it immediately. It was loud, really loud, but after a while I hardly noticed, I got used to it. We had a good team warm-up, but it was hot out there. I must have had three large water bottles of electrolytes. I was hungry.

Back to the dressing room. Mel addressed the matter of the American men's team. She said, "Our men's team is here, too. They're up in the press box, and they want you to know they're here cheering, too."

The atmosphere in the dressing room was loose, yet serious. Some players sat with their eyes closed. Some chatted and made jokes. Others fiddled with their equipment. Everyone, though, was chomping at the bit, wanting the game to get underway. I used the time to say a few things: "Let's have a good start, girls. The first five minutes is key." We had music cranked, with Piper controlling the iPod.

GAME TIME. THE FIRST PERIOD. Holy cow, I don't know what happened. We had penalties—at one point we had to kill a five-on-three. The TSN Turning Point of the game was probably the shot I blocked, when we were two short, to get the puck out of the zone. I played a lot of minutes in that first period. I was pretty gassed from the adrenalin and the effort of playing short-handed.

We scored, perhaps thirty seconds after killing off those penalties! Young Poulin! Botterill made such a nice play to get the puck to her, and Poulin just ripped it over Jessie Vetter, the American goaltender. Vetter wasn't expecting a release like that. We then got a second goal shortly after, off the faceoff. The puck came to Poulin again, and she beat Vetter, low this time. I didn't even see the goals. I was too busy trying to recover after killing those penalties.

After we scored the second goal, and having made it through that first period without allowing the Americans a goal, I knew Szabados was going to shut the door and not allow anything.

We came off the ice with a two-goal lead after twenty minutes. Mike Babcock, Lindy Ruff, and the other coaches from the men's team greeted us in the hallway. I think they had heard what the Americans had done to us so they got out and lined the hall, cheering: "Way to go, girls, keep it going."

There was almost a sense of relief in the dressing room after that first period. The room was noisy, a lot of the girls were talking: "Nice penalty kill! Great shot, Poulin! Nice block, Wick! Great play!" There was a sense of urgency and purpose. Mel came in and, calmly, matter-of-factly said, "Great start. We're doing what we need to do. Stick with the plan. Let's take it to them."

More penalties in the second period. The Americans came on strong. They played really well. But they couldn't get a goal. I was so tired when I came off the ice after the second period. So many penalties to kill. There was another five-on-three. That was a huge penalty kill. They ended up out-shooting us 13–10 in that period, but we stood our ground. I'd played about twenty minutes after two periods. I was pretty gassed but loving it. There was nowhere else in the world I wanted to be. I drank more fluid, more electrolytes, just trying to keep myself going.

After forty minutes everyone came into the dressing room a little looser. We were still up 2–0. There was a lot of chatter. I was pretty vocal through much of the game, and at that point I said, "It comes down to the little things. Let's keep doing those little things, the important things, and not get too far ahead of ourselves."

There was considerable excitement, a sense we had the game in hand. But the veterans on the team knew it was still far from that. We had to keep going and remain positive. Mel came in and didn't say much. She kept her words simple, positive. She appeared very relaxed, and I think she made an effort to show that she believed in us.

I don't think we had another penalty in that third period. What surprised us was that the Americans just sat back and didn't push any further. We pushed. We kept going at them, and we were by far the better team. The clock was ticking down. When it hit the

ten-minute mark I was thinking, "Geez, get this game over with."
There were moments when I just wanted to win so bad it was almost
paralyzing. The clock couldn't tick down fast enough. At the four-
minute mark someone said, "They don't have anything left." At the
two-minute mark I absolutely knew there was no way they would
get two goals in the next two minutes. From that point we wanted
to make sure Szabby got her shutout. She played phenomenally.

It was hard to keep the lid on celebrating until the game was
completely over. With about forty-six seconds left, Apps, Piper,
and I were thinking, "Just keep the puck in their end, just jam
it, get the puck moving, get it low, I'm going to be the high man."
And all the time we couldn't help but watch the clock. Jenny
Potter, one of the American veterans, skated up the ice with about
seven seconds left. I was staring at her, she was staring at me. It
was a weird moment. I knew there was nothing left for us to do
and I knew they had nothing left. I turned around and, with seven
seconds left, even though the game was still technically going on, I
started celebrating with the crowd. Then it was over! We all rushed
out to jump on Szabby. I got totally caught up in the moment.

THE ENTIRE TEAM PLAYED WELL, we did what we had to do. We got
the job done. And it was a whole team effort. I was totally, totally
proud of the team. And I was happy for Mel, Peter, Doug, and all
the staff who worked so hard. Canada 2, USA 0!

Tomas brought Noah down, and he joined me on the ice. Before
the game he had said, "Mom, this time if we win can I come out on
the ice?" So there he was, sharing this great moment with me.

Bob Nicholson was standing on our bench with Johnny Misley,
and I said, "Thank you guys, we did it! Thanks for believing in us."
Bob was really emotional. Robin McDonald, our doctors, everybody was celebrating. I also felt it was important to just take a
moment, look around and take in the crowd. Wow, that crowd was

going crazy. It was so loud, and all I could see was a sea of red and white. I wasn't able to locate my family until later, when we got our medals.

Dick Pound presented the medals. Four years ago he also presented them to us in Torino. I had heard rumours that it was going to be Wayne Gretzky presenting them, but it turned out to be Dick Pound. They played the anthem. Such a proud moment, the crowd was going wild. Then it was over. We lingered on that ice for a good forty-five minutes, taking pictures, skating for the crowd, waving at people, giving them some photo ops. Boom, it was time to walk off. Weird, like walking off into the sunset.

I WALKED OFF, and it was boom, all right. The media! I spent an hour talking with reporters, fielding various versions of: "Hayley, how does it feel to win? Are you going to retire? Should women's hockey be in the Olympics? What about what Jacques Rogge said about the blowouts?"

Just as an aside, I think what he said was just fine, actually, and not a bad thing for our game if it makes the federations wake up and pay attention to what's going on.

It took a long time to run that gauntlet. But at the end of the media line, there were Stephen Harper and Gordon Campbell. The prime minister was wearing a jersey, my jersey! They both came into our dressing room. I find them both to be very supportive of our team and our game. You can say what you want about the prime minister, maybe he is a little dry, but his comment was, "Hey, every medal is great at the Olympics, but we know which medals Canada is so passionate about. You guys, being a hockey team, you did it under a lot of pressure and expectation from a nation." That was a fantastic thing for him to say.

Our celebration was well under way by the time I returned to the dressing room. Everybody had cigars, there was champagne—a totally normal hockey tradition. I handed a fresh cigar, not lit, to Gordon Campbell, and another to the prime minister, who looked at it and said, "What's this?" I said, "That's for you, enjoy it." He laughed. There was no way, whatsoever, they were going to smoke those things!

Given the events that would unfold in the next twenty-four hours, I was sure happy they didn't. A good move!

They stayed for a few more minutes, had a few pictures taken and then they left. We partied. We reminisced about the year. Doping control was in there trying to take people out, and there we were thinking, "Honestly, you guys, chill out." I sat in my equipment for a few minutes, finally took it off, and got ready to have a shower.

Nike had sent in a box of golden shoes for each player, and a nice sweater to wear. We put them on and decided that, as a team, we would wear the golden shoes and sweater which would later get us in trouble. But at the time it was cool. Then a lot of the girls decided to go back out on the ice—at this point it was about two hours after the end of the game. They went back out and proceeded to take pictures, with cigars and beer in hand. Ouch! That was a bad move.

Canadian Press and Associated Press were still in the building. They took some shots of the girls on the ice, still celebrating. No fans were in the rink. It was just media. CP put it out on the wire. AP put it out on the wire.

Well, that started a storm. The IOC came back and said it didn't condone such activity. It started a crazy, crazy flurry of banter, that's basically what it was.

At one point I was the only one left in our dressing room— thank God, in a way! I had just spent an hour with the media and I just wanted to sit and have a drink. I took a shower, got changed, and the girls came in from the ice. I grabbed a bite to eat, maybe three pieces of sushi and a bit of champagne in the players' lounge, and then went over to the Hockey House with Peter Jensen. My family was over there, and we only had forty-five minutes before the team had to go to the International Broadcast Centre.

Danielle was the first person I saw at the Hockey House. I bawled my eyes out. Then I saw the rest of the gang. The tears really hit me. When I was on the ice, I didn't feel any of that emotion. It was more like: "Yes, we did it. Thank God it's over. It's such a relief to be in Canada, to get this over and done with, and to win."

I shed a lot of tears and had a wonderful visit with them. Donald Sutherland came by and congratulated us. Noah got his picture with him. I asked Donald if he had any contacts for *The Ellen DeGeneres Show*—Noah has wanted to go watch a taping. He said he would try to help.

From that point it was just chaos; people were everywhere, autograph seekers, pictures, cheering. What a crazy but fun time!

Our whole team took a bus to the International Broadcast Centre to meet with Brian Williams. By the time we arrived, we started to hear rumblings about a couple of things. One issue was the drinking and smoking on the ice, by Poulin in particular, and our team's post-game celebration in general, which was ridiculous. It took place two hours after the game. Poulin, the poor kid is eighteen and legal in her own province. If she wants to have a celebratory cigar and beer, it's not a big deal! But some of our staff were freaking out. They said she should not have had any alcohol in her hand.

And there was another issue. We wore our white Nike jackets, and you're only supposed to wear HBC clothing on television. So HBC and the Canadian Olympic Committee were upset. Oops.

I had to answer a few questions from Brian Williams: How do you feel having to defend your sport? How hard is it to get here? What about the Canada-U.S. rivalry? Basically it was Szabados,

Agosta, and I who spoke for the team. He also talked to Becky Kellar, whose kids were there with her.

We went back to the Hockey House and just partied with our friends. After that we ended up at another bar with the rest of the team and finally shut it down at about 4 AM. It was a crazy night.

What a whirlwind! Our final stop was the McDonald's in the athletes' village. The McDonald's people let me come into the back area and make myself my own cheeseburger. I grabbed some fries, some Chicken McNuggets, served a couple of people—hilarious! I saw the Finnish head coach in there. He congratulated us. The Finns were so happy that they had won a bronze medal. It was a big deal for them.

Scott Moir and some of the other skaters were also there, and I chatted with him. He's a real card. Tessa is quiet, a small-town girl. Scott is a boisterous, funny guy—exactly what people saw on TV.

I'm glad it's over. More than anything, it's a relief. It's a burden off the shoulders. For months it's been a huge weight, and now it's gone. We can just relax.

FEBRUARY 26

Talk about a huge weight. That gold medal is heavy!

Everywhere I went today, I ran into people offering various versions of "Congratulations!" Wherever I go I have my medal. If I go through security I pull it out for the scanners to see. I let them enjoy the moment. It only takes five or six minutes. They stand there day after day, doing their jobs—the medal is a piece of them, a piece of Canada. It makes me happy to share it with them, with volunteers, with the police.

I met up with Noah and Tomas. Noah was so cute, he wanted to see the medal. I shared the moment with some parents in the Petro-Canada Lounge at the hotel. I took Noah for lunch while Tomas packed things up. At one point I had to go to the bathroom, and Noah said, "Don't worry about it, Mom, I'll watch your gold medal!" So he was really into it. Tomas said Noah was actually nervous in the third period and excited for us to win. I think he finally got this one.

Oh yes, I got a call back about the *Ellen Show*. Someone was going to work on it. The problem is they have to make an exception for Noah because they don't allow anyone under fourteen in the studio. I hope they make an exception so that, down the road, I can take him down for a show and a couple of days at Disneyland.

The world is your oyster when you win an Olympic gold medal. Well, for a few hours or maybe days, you can almost do anything!

But there was still work to do. Poulin, Agosta, myself, and Szabados had to go to the International Broadcast Centre again. We spent three hours talking to the media. I answered one basic question—how does it feel to win—and the rest of the time I answered questions about the drinking on the ice, the fiasco, and if I was going to retire after these Games.

By the way, I'm not. So I just kept saying, "No, I'm not retiring."

I could not believe the questions. The media was really looking to spin a yarn about the post-game celebration on the ice with the beer and cigars. But a couple of reporters said, "If this was the men's team this would never happen." It's true. It's complete and utter garbage. I just won a gold medal, and I have to stand there and defend this? It's unfathomable.

It was a strange situation. Do we celebrate, do we feel bad, do we feel ashamed, embarrassed? There were so many emotions. This really dampened our excitement. Some of the girls were a bit embarrassed by what had happened. They didn't have to be.

I went to bat for them in the media, the papers. I said, "There's no story here. We celebrated like any other hockey team. In the history of the game, NHL, Stanley Cup, the same thing goes on—spraying champagne all over the place, having cigars, a beer. Get a grip, people. It's really crap, it's sexist, and it's wrong to make an issue of it."

The IOC had been the first people to comment on it, and they handled it completely the wrong way. We saw them backtrack later and say there is no story here. That was good. We're people. We're human beings. At the end of the day we're not the perfect little angels like they might have us pinned up to be.

I was a bit deflated after defending all of that for a few hours. It was hard to watch young Poulin go through the process. Here's a kid who scored two goals in the Olympic final, and she has to defend why and how she was celebrating! Agosta and I went to the village McDonald's again. I eat at McDonald's maybe twice in four years, and it's at the Olympics. Comical. For months, even years, leading up to this you treat your body so well. Then you want to just let loose? But that's what I did. I had a cheeseburger, fries, a Coke.

I came back and ran into Joannie Rochette. While we were celebrating our gold medal last night, she went out and won a bronze medal under the most difficult of circumstances. No one would have blamed her if she opted not to compete here. Not only did she compete, she was bravery and grace on ice, and despite what must have been a terrible week she came away with a medal. I said to her, "Such a performance, you should be so proud of yourself." She said, "Sometimes I'm really calm, sometimes I'm sad and want to cry, sometimes I'm just fine." I think being here at the Olympics has helped keep her kind of even keel, being around the other athletes. I think the hardest thing for her will be when she leaves the athletes' village. When the distractions are gone she will have to really deal with everything. But what a gutsy performance! Our whole team is proud of her.

THE DAY BROUGHT HOME the highs and lows of the Olympics. We were tired but definitely on a high. The day also illustrated how the difference between winning and losing can be a fraction of an inch, a fraction of a second. In the women's curling final Cheryl Bernard literally missed a shot by a fraction of an inch in the tenth end. It opened up a door, boom, she had to settle for silver. That's what we didn't want to happen with us against the U.S. If they got one goal, they might get two.

General Mills gave Szabados and I some tickets to the men's semifinal. We entered the rink down below and saw Wayne Gretzky watching the last bit of curling on television. We saw Miroslav Satan and Ziggy Palffy getting ready for the game, a lot of Slovaks walking around. We went up to the suite and mixed and mingled with the General Mills folks. We watched the game for a couple of periods then decided to go to the CAN Fund Athlete House. The rest of our team was there, watching the game with friends and family. Canada won 3-2, setting up a rematch with the United States in Sunday's gold medal game. Talk about an Olympic finale!

I was exhausted. I could barely keep my eyes open. I came back to the village and visited with Mel for about an hour—we reminisced about the game, the year, the season. What a day! What a week! What a season!

FEBRUARY 27

What can I say, other than what a great ride it has been. I am totally, totally exhausted. I'm glad it's over.

The Games are winding down. People in the village are out later, the McDonald's line is a little longer. I just want to enjoy what's left of the Games, and rest. I have an appearance to make at the Cheerios Cheer Wall, an installation downtown where messages from fans to athletes are posted. But other than that I want to lay low, just remember these Games and enjoy our team's accomplishment after what was a long, hard season.

By the end of yesterday, I was becoming irritated with so many people wanting photographs and signatures. That's when you know you need to go home—when you're tired and you don't have the patience anymore. Then you have to get away from the public. Everyone is just being sincere, they want to congratulate you, but at some point it becomes too much and you have to know when to shut it down. It's safe to say that during the past two weeks we ran into most of the distractions on the list we made at the pre-Olympic camp in Jasper.

I don't know how Wayne Gretzky does it. What I went through yesterday is what he goes through every single day. For many of Canada's athletes public life will never be the same after these Games.

But despite the public attention and scrutiny I must say there was never a time that I felt unsafe. We were very secure, yet I never felt an overbearing presence of police or security people, nor did their vigilance lapse as the Games went on. In past Olympics that has, at times, been the case—as the days went on there were lulls, people became more flexible about the rules. But here the security was steady, very consistent the whole time. But they weren't absolutely rigid, either. When Szabados and I had to get to the arena in a hurry, in the pouring rain, two very nice cops gave us a ride through the back streets.

It has been an amazing journey, an emotional journey. It was a very difficult year for me in many ways. Winning the gold medal took a lot of effort. People don't understand what goes into something like this. They don't get it. They say, "The women's hockey team just rolled through the tournament and won the gold medal." You don't roll through something and win if you don't work your butt off to separate yourself from everyone else. That's what we did, every day for the past seven months. The legacy of all this is that over a hundred thousand girls will be playing the game of hockey in 2010. If there are more than eighty thousand now, you can bet there will be even more after this. What a great thing!

I am annoyed at the media questions. I still have to defend the stupid cigar and champagne thing and defend why women's hockey should be in the Olympics. It seems those are the only two things reporters want to talk about. I want to talk about our team.

Earlier in the Games there was talk about how the Own the Podium program hadn't really panned out for Canadian athletes, that it wasn't a success. Perhaps that thinking has changed. Going into tomorrow, Canada has thirteen gold medals, a lot of silvers and bronzes, and a lot of fourth-place finishes. And look at the way Canada has responded to the Olympics! To me, these Games were a success, and OTP has been a success. It was worth every cent, and I certainly feel it was crucial for our victory. OTP money allowed us to have more camps, including specific position camps like our goalie camp, and we reaped the benefit of more and better sport science.

I don't want our Olympics to be over, but I'm also glad they are. It's difficult to relax here, because wherever we go we are in the public eye. It will be nice to get out of the fishbowl. We accomplished what we set out to do here. Our job is done.

We won gold—at home.

FEBRUARY 28

Today is the last day of the Games. It's hard to believe we'll be going home tomorrow after so many years of planning, after thinking about the Olympics every day this past year.

This morning our team went to the CTV studios and did a meeting of the medallists with Brian Williams, Lisa Laflamme, and Michael Landsberg. It was a great idea to get us all together, and almost all the medallists were there—except the men's hockey team, of course, because they were still slated to play the U.S. for gold in the last competitive event of these Games. Later, Stephan Moccio, one of the two men who composed the "I Believe" song, came on the set and he played it for us.

Jennifer Heil and I talked about what it feels like to be an individual competing at the Olympics versus being in a team sport. She had a lot of pressure on her as an individual athlete and as a defending Olympic champion, and in the end there was really no one out there to help and support her once she started her run. She had to go down that hill and do it all by herself. In fact, she told me, in her final run she had gone into her jump a little sideways, and the athlete who beat her skied the race of her life. That's sport—the smallest of details can make the biggest difference.

We had to be back on a bus by 11:30 AM to go to the men's game. The downtown area was jumping. There was so much anticipation. The streets were clogged with people waving flags, singing, chanting. We got to the stadium and went right to the front of the security line even though there was a long lineup to get in. I said to some of the girls, "We're the women's hockey team. We're not going to go to the back of the line and miss out on the start of this game." We found a very nice police officer who escorted us through the VIP line and into the rink. We made our way to the athletes' seating area—second level, first row, great seats just across from the USA bench.

Wow, what an atmosphere. But the game, to me, seemed initially quieter than the start of our game. People were nervous. Canada went up 1–0 in the first, then 2–0, then the U.S. got on the scoreboard midway through the second to make it 2–1.

Everyone on our team was exhausted. I looked over at one point, and the girls were slumped in their seats, completely out of gas. It was neat because we were sitting right across from the U.S. women's team, like we were in Salt Lake. And it was a rematch of the men's teams that played for gold in Salt Lake. The Canadians scored, and we went crazy then looked over at them; the Americans scored, and they looked over at us.

I actually thought Canada had it with about five minutes to go, then the play started going back and forth, and with seconds left the U.S. scored to tie it up. The whole building went silent. I thought, "This is destiny." At the time I was texting back and forth with a friend in Calgary, and I said, "Sidney's going to get the winner. I bet you five hundred bucks!" I glanced at the American women. They were so excited, and I thought, "It's going to be really sweet to see their reaction when we score in overtime."

Sure enough, about seven minutes into the overtime Sidney Crosby got the winner. It almost felt like it was scripted out. Jarome, Sidney, Scott Niedermayer, to name a few, had struggled early in the tournament, but it wasn't as if they played bad. Great players elevate themselves to another level when it really matters. That's exactly what Jarome did, he popped the puck out, a lucky break off the referee. Then Sid picked it up and surprised Miller on a fairly weak-angled shot. The puck went in. Crazy!

I was sitting beside Tessa Bonhomme and we hugged, it was high-fives all around our team. Then I looked at the crowd, I just wanted to watch people celebrate. The building absolutely erupted, bedlam and jubilation. And again, I thought, "This was destiny, this was meant to be. What a storybook ending."

We stood, we sang the anthem, and the electricity of the crowd and the moment buzzed all around. The guys looked relieved. They were excited, but they also realized what a moment it was in history. Corey Perry grabbed a giant Canadian flag and passed it through the team. Sidney got it all twisted up, and we howled, it looked so funny. They were laughing at themselves and trying to get it untwisted.

It was over. They disappeared into the tunnel. I said to the girls, "Let's go downstairs. If people are mingling, we'll say our congratulations to the guys, but if the dressing room is closed then we'll keep moving." So we worked our way down. The media scrum was incredible, huge. A few of the players were still doing interviews but the dressing room was closed, so we kept going, kept walking, and carried on back to the athletes' village.

We only had twenty minutes to get changed, we had to get ready for the closing ceremonies. But the excitement and honking of horns! People were screaming in the streets. People were coming up to us—I had to put my hood up and hide a little bit so as not to get stopped, because we had so very little time to get back to the village. The city was going berserk, and I wondered if that high would ever end.

THE TANK WAS PRETTY MUCH on empty by the time I went to the closing ceremonies. Instead of putting everyone in GM Place they had all the athletes go through the airlock and into the tunnel to await marching into the stadium. Volunteers were asking for pictures and autographs. At one point I went over to Becky Kellar and said, "I think I'm going to faint." I was so spent.

But there was a great atmosphere within our Canadian team, all the athletes from different sports mixing and mingling. Colleen Sostorics was comparing biceps with Lascelles Brown, the bobsledder. I stood with the women bobsledders for a bit. They're pretty fun-loving. I see them around the gym at the Oval in Calgary. They train really hard. It was great for them because they don't get the attention that comes the way of speed skaters or hockey players, so for them to win was extra special.

I saw Scott Niedermayer and asked him why he decided to walk—I think he was the only guy on the men's team to walk in the closing ceremonies. He said he decided to join us because he really wanted the experience, he'd never been to a closing ceremony.

Later, I sat up against a wall with Kellar and Sostorics. My legs were just throbbing. Done. Totally spent.

Finally we walked in. The atmosphere wasn't as electric as it was for the opening, a little more subdued, definitely different. I could sense in the crowd great support and appreciation but also a sense of sadness or disappointment that it was all coming to an end. Also, for the closing, we didn't really walk in as separate nations—our flagbearers came out ahead and then the athletes came in jumbled together—our team entered mixed in with France. It was much less formal than the opening.

Joannie Rochette was our closing ceremonies flagbearer. We had seen her earlier in the day at the CTV studios for the gathering of the medallists, and she didn't seem to waver, she was very solid. She handled everything so well, very resilient, very strong. Everybody was surprised. I think people expected her to be a lot more emotional and have breakdowns. I'm sure she had her moments in private. But publicly, in front of the media and all us athletes, she was consistently stoic as she prepared to compete.

We walked in, sat down, and had to put on ponchos to blend into the crowd. I really didn't want to do it because it was so hot in there. At each seat there was a kit with lights and props to wave, but I didn't participate in any of that. For a while I just sat there, staring straight ahead, thinking, "I really need to get out of here and go to my bed."

The ceremony was a bit off the wall. There was Michael J. Fox, William Shatner, and by the time it got to Catherine O'Hara we started looking at each other, saying, "This is different!" I felt we were blowing our horn a bit more than I've expected us to as Canadians. But we had a great Olympics, so why not? Then they brought out the RCMP, the beavers, the hockey players, a lot of cliché images of Canada. I whispered to one of the girls, "I wonder if the rest of the world is getting this?" We understood what it was all about. It was funny, sort of cheesy. It wasn't my favourite closing—I loved the opening here, it was beautiful and elegant. The closing seemed more cartoonish, comical, but maybe that was what they were trying to do. But also, when you are fatigued, your patience and attention span aren't what they might be.

I sat there staring into space half the time, reminiscing about my whole Games experience. And I kept thinking to myself, "My God, tomorrow I go home."

We filed onto the floor when the official part of the program ended. Alanis Morissette, Simple Plan, a couple of other bands took to the stage. We just mingled with the athletes of the world. I traded my closing ceremony jacket for a "See You In Sochi" jersey—kind of funny because throughout the Games everyone was asking me if I was going to retire, was I going to be in Sochi? So I thought it would be appropriate to wear that jersey. I ran into Mel, and she liked my Sochi jersey so much she went off and did the same thing.

I didn't stay much longer. I needed to go to the Hockey House to sign a few more items for a silent auction. Mel needed to go there as well, so we walked over together. We had to cross a street that was against the flow of traffic, right where the prime minister's motor- cade was supposed to come through. One of the police officers put her hand up as if to say we couldn't go there, then she recognized us and volunteered to escort us.

We talked as we walked, and it turned out she was on the Canadian volleyball team in 1976. She said the Games had come a long way from her day, they didn't have the support that we have, things have changed and grown through the years. She said she hadn't been able to see anything because she worked through these entire Games, just manning her post. She wasn't even really supposed to talk to anybody. I felt for her. She was emotional, too. At one point she said, "This is my Olympic moment, walking you guys to the Hockey House." I felt I had to do something for this woman so I gave her my closing ceremonies hat, Mel and I both signed it and gave it to her.

She got kind of teary-eyed and said, "I'm not supposed to accept anything." I laughed and said, "Forget it. It's over! What are they going to do, send you home?" So she stuck it inside her jacket. It was a special little moment.

BACK TO THE VILLAGE! What does a final-day party look like in the athletes' village? The Canadian team party was in the bottom of our building, in the parking garage. It was actually really neat— they had pizza and beer, it was like an old-fashioned garage party. We stayed there for a while then some of the women's team went upstairs, one of the teammates had a bottle of champagne and we cracked it open, sitting on the floor of the athletes' lounge. Some of the girls were packing, some were just watching TV, some of us just lay there, exhausted.

Finally, a few of us decided to go to the party in the main athletes' building in the village—it turned out to be really fun. There were about fifty or sixty Canadian athletes there. Sidney Crosby, Patrice Bergeron, Shea Weber, some of the men's team were there. They chose not to walk in the closing but they weren't actually leaving until the next day. So they, and we, celebrated with the rest of the world's athletes.

Tomorrow we all go our separate ways.

MARCH 1

I woke up at about 8:30 AM and made my way to the dining hall, where I ate with Kevin Martin and his team, the newly crowned Olympic kings of curling. There was sadness in the air. At the start of the Games, the dining hall was crowded, buzzing with activity and excitement. As the games progressed the atmosphere developed a certain rhythm coinciding with the schedule or a particular sport or group of athletes. When we ate a pre-game meal the hall tended to be empty. But when we came back it would be full. But as the Games went on it became quieter. Today as I sat with the curlers, just a few athletes were milling in and out. The dining hall is really the heart of the village, the pulse. But by this morning that beat was nearly still.

On the way back I played a little street hockey in the village, then I grabbed a cart, went up to my room, and packed. It was a bit nostalgic, pulling pictures off the walls, at the same time rushing to get everything done. We received so much stuff at these Olympics. I didn't have enough room to bring it all home, so I was stressed trying to get everything into my bags, trying to decide what to leave behind. At one point I had Szabby standing on a bag while I tried to zip it up. Botts was in there helping. I came back with five separate bags and two backpacks and three bigger ones, and I still had to leave some stuff behind. By then my attitude was: "Just shove it in the bag. Just get it in and figure it out when you get home." Through it all there was a current of exhaustion and emotion.

There were also conflicting senses: thank God it's over, and oh my God, what's next?

I carefully packed some of the special things—cards I had been given, the little Amidala from Noah, my dog tags. I wanted to make sure those things were put in a safe place so I wouldn't lose them. I just shoved other stuff in the bags. It took me an hour to pack, clean up the room a bit, and I went and loaded it all on the bus. Then we left.

Leaving the room certainly wasn't the same as arriving and setting up. When I arrived at the village three weeks ago I had a sense of anticipation. Today was just chaos coupled with fatigue.

THE VILLAGE WAS EERIE, quite quiet, when we left. It was a grey day, and cool. We left at about one o'clock, and a lot of people had already gone. It was sad and nostalgic to say goodbye to the volunteers and drive through the city, knowing the next time I come to Vancouver it will not be the same.

The response to these Games was amazing and unparalleled. I do wish I could have just blended into those wild crowds some nights, just to be a part of it all. There were a couple of nights that we did go out, tried to be fans, but usually we'd be recognized. To be an average joe and just go to the Games would have been terrific. When you're an athlete, one part that sucks about the Games is you don't actually see the Olympics. You're in it, like the eye of a hurricane, and you're not necessarily aware of the whirlwind of activity and events going on all around.

I tried to keep myself in my little bubble through much of the Games, but there was no escaping its impact on Canada and Canadians. I have never seen such an outpouring of emotion and enthusiasm in the Canadian public. Prior to the opening ceremonies there was sense of optimism and enthusiasm, but then everything exploded when Alexandre Bilodeau won Canada's first gold medal, and the mood just escalated from there. It was like a collective snowball that started to roll until it just carried everyone in its wake. Canadians were saying, "Hey, we can be good and we can show it. And not only are we good, we are really good. We've got fourteen gold medals."

But the celebrations didn't get out of hand. There was certainly a lot of noise and energy and interest, but the mood never morphed into something that was arrogant or boastful. I think VANOC tried to bring that out in the closing ceremonies, playing up the national pride and acknowledging that the way we were at these Games is who we are as a people. We're nice, we get along. There were no riots or crazy things during the Games, just the odd protest. As Canadians we do the job, we take pride in it, and we celebrate really well. And what we saw in Vancouver was a lot of people who were not afraid to celebrate. Ironically, when we won the gold medal and the whole flap ensued about the champagne and cigars, it was funny to hear the Canadian public react to the media's disapproval of what the team had done. The average Canadian, I think, loved it.

There were, in fact, many things that resonated with Canadians at the Games. Alex's gold medal win was historic and special, but equally compelling was the love and respect he showed for his brother, Frédéric, and the unrelenting cheerfulness he exhibited in the crush of attention that enveloped him after his win. Joannie Rochette's grace and strength in grief was moving and inspiring, her efforts on the ice a poignant tribute to her mother. Who couldn't appreciate the unbridled enthusiasm of Jon Montgomery as he celebrated his skeleton win? Who wasn't stirred by the beauty and depth of Virtue and Moir's fairy tale on ice?

And Canadian hockey fans have two gold medals to savour!

People wanted so badly for our athletes to do well. Sometimes that can get misconstrued as pressure. But it was just a genuine "want," almost willing the athletes to do well. In fact, the Canadian public was probably responsible for a few extra medals. Their emotion and support gave us wings.

And the superb organization continued right through to the end. When we arrived at Vancouver International Airport, they were ready for us. They walked us right through security, way faster than checking in on a normal day. These Games were absolutely organized, from top to bottom. They really were superb.

BACK TO CALGARY. I got on the plane, and there was Beckie Scott sitting in the first row. She was pregnant, and I got a picture of her with the medal on her stomach. We chatted the whole way home. We landed in Calgary, and there was some local media, not as much as when some athletes got back on an earlier flight. There was a little boy there from Medicine Hat, on his way to Disneyland as part of the Make-A-Wish Foundation, so I put my medal around his neck. My mom and dad were there and they brought me home.

I came through the door, and the house was absolutely quiet, Tomas and Noah weren't home. I sat on the steps, just sat there in silence for ten or fifteen minutes. I thought, "I can't believe it's over."

It was strange to come home to such a quiet place after three weeks of Olympic bedlam. I had a shower, grabbed a bite to eat, and went to bed. That was it. I felt exhausted. Done. Spent. Happy. Satisfied. And a little bit sad that it was all over.

MARCH 18

People continue to ask about my medal and want to see it. It's smaller than the Torino medal but bigger than the ones from Nagano and Salt Lake. It's the most beautiful of my medals, and it's extremely heavy. It seems I have to take it out with me every day, because everywhere I go people like to see it. I went over to say hello to Jane and Marty Gelinas—he played in the NHL for a long time—and I showed it to them. I've taken it to Noah's school and to his swimming program so that all the little Dino swimmers could have a look.

We had a big party here on the 12th. Two hundred and fifty people showed up—friends, neighbours, family from Calgary and the area. We rented a room in the basement of Ceili's, a pub here in Calgary. Aurelio made an awesome three-by-three-foot cake that looked like the gold medal. We had a great time, and it was a fun way to let family and friends look at the medal, to bring them all together at the same time.

I don't mind taking the medal with me wherever I go. After a while it becomes a part of you, like an extra appendage. When you're in this situation you have to understand you're going to get the same questions over and over. How heavy is it? Is it real gold?

For some people this may be the first and only time they will ever see an Olympic gold medal, so you have to be gracious and respond to the same questions over and over. And you have to remember that all of this is not going to last forever.

A third gold medal. I look at them all now and think, "There are a lot of memories wrapped up in a lot of metal."

I have yet to step back on the ice. I've had offers to play, but I have no interest to be on the ice right now. It's a bit strange to have the national team season end with the final at the Olympics. After the Games, some of the athletes went back to compete in Europe. The figure skaters have their World Championships coming up. The alpine skiers are still racing, as are the speed skaters.

The second day I was home, I woke up and thought, "Wow, what am I going to do now? I don't *have* to go to the gym." I wouldn't call it a letdown. It's nice not to have to go to the gym, or get up and practise, or play games. In this first week I did a bit of a run, played some squash, and that was it. I guess it's kind of like a relaxed exhaustion, coupled with a feeling of satisfaction.

I've received so many e-mails, texts, invitations, and opportunities to speak. I'm hiring Ceilidh, who handles my PR and communication, full-time to help me manage. And there's still the day-to-day stuff, getting Noah back on track for school. I don't think I've stopped this first week. I've barely slept.

One thing I have done is purge my house. I threw out twenty-one bags of junk and gave away another ten bags of stuff. I just felt like one chapter is now done, the next one has to begin. So let's just get the house clean. I've just had this huge desire to get organized. During the last year I had to put a lot of things off so now, I'm purging, cleaning.

I LOOK BACK AT the last seven months, and it hardly seems like it was real—the travel, the Midget AAA games, my injured back, pneumonia in January, going to the Games, and the whirlwind that life has been ever since. It was an incredible experience.

It was also a hell of a year in the sense that it was, at times, hell. Some days I don't know how we all did it. I've learned I need to have more personal time. Be at home. Spend more quality time with my son. Do things I want to do and find a direction I might want to move in.

When I look back I also see the past year as a great year. The reason we won the gold medal? Preparation! There were days we might whine and complain about the schedule being hard, but no other country in the world was working as hard. We came prepared as a team and as individuals. And on Any Given Day, which is our team motto, I'm proud that we found a way.

EPILOGUE

Time is a strange thing. It moves fast or slow, depending on your situation. The one constant for me is that there never seems to be enough of it.

The weeks following the Olympics were filled with interview requests, appearances, public speaking opportunities. Then, finally, I was able to get some downtime—a holiday in New York City with Tomas and Noah and a trip to Los Angeles with Noah to visit Universal Studios and *The Ellen DeGeneres Show.*

Winning an Olympic gold medal always draws a certain amount of attention. But winning gold in Canada really intensified that exposure. While walking around New York City, I was stopped at least twenty times by Canadians. I was in a department store, and a woman from Windsor came up and said, "Hey, can I get a picture?" We went to a Broadway show, *The Lion King,* and met a woman from White Rock and talked about the Olympics. At Universal Studios we ran into a family from Calgary, and they all wanted a picture.

The Olympic attention culminated a few weeks later when Montreal feted Canada's Olympic athletes with a huge parade. So much support, so much energy—the day helped us relive the great feelings and excitement we enjoyed in February in Vancouver. In May I was honoured to return home to Shaunavon for a day of celebration billed as Hayley's Golden Hat Trick. Noah came with me, and it was wonderful to share the day with old friends and to be back home, where I received so much support early in my hockey career. Although I've lived in Calgary for twenty years, the Shaunavon community played a big part in who I am today.

LOOKING BACK I THINK our 2010 hockey team had the most depth and was perhaps the most talented of any women's Team Canada. It was not the most experienced, nor perhaps the closest or most united team, but it was definitely the fittest and most skilled to ever represent Canada in Olympic women's hockey. I'm proud we didn't succumb to the pressure or expectations. I also enjoyed the team's metamorphosis from a group that doubted its ability to perform under pressure to a team that believed and found an inner confidence and strength to win.

As for my individual play, I probably could have scored more goals against teams like Slovakia. But my game plan changed, and I became more of a playmaker than a goal scorer, finishing the Olympic tournament with eleven points in the five games. My concern in those early games wasn't to get points, it was to move the puck, to make the players I was playing with feel better and get on a roll. Maybe I should have been more selfish at times; I probably could have had three or four more goals. But we didn't need more goals. We needed good habits. Good leadership. In the game against Slovakia, we needed me to play the way I was going to need to play against the U.S.

Shirley Cameron, a very good friend who played in the 1990 World Championships, said, "I know you didn't get any points in the final game, Hayley, but it was probably the best and most complete game I've seen you play in your career. You blocked shots, you made plays, you remained composed." Her words meant a lot to me.

Poise, composure, trust—those were what I wanted to inject into my play. Our team was young, we had seven Olympic rookies, so I had to take on some of the dirty work. This win is perhaps the proudest accomplishment of my career.

When I look back on our preparation, yeah, there were days when the coaches pushed the envelope. There were days when we thought, "This might be too much. We could use one less game here or there."

But then you read and hear the media saying, "You guys are blowing everybody away. You guys are way better." It's simple. We work harder. We prepare smarter. That's what we do. We do it better than any other country. At the same time, they say it's not good for women's hockey. I say, "No, it's great for women's hockey. Look at how good our team is. Look at the athleticism, the skill level. The rest of the world needs to do the same thing!"

If Russia, Sweden, or Finland inject more resources into their female hockey programs, I'd consider going over and helping them when I finish my playing days. Why not? It would be a great challenge. Ideally I'd like to work with the International Ice Hockey Federation to help with women's hockey around the world.

Women's hockey is not in any danger of being pulled from the Olympics. It's competitive and it's improving. Canada pushed the game to another level because we wanted so badly to win gold in our own country. It mattered so much. It would be great if the rest of the world could develop the same passion for women's hockey as we have in Canada. Then we might see the same type of preparation and performance from them.

The countdown to Sochi has begun. Change is inevitable in the years between Olympics, and it may be that as much as half of the team that won women's gold in Vancouver will have retired or moved on by 2014. Life goes on, for my teammates and for me.

I'M NOW FOCUSING ON my tournament, which takes place in Burnaby in November 2010. The Samsung Wickenheiser International

Women's Hockey Festival will include thirty-two teams from around the world, from peewee to senior level. And it's more than a hockey tournament. There will be seminars about nutrition, equipment, education, parents in the game. It's a forum to educate, to grow the game and promote it in other countries. For me it's about doing my part to help develop women's hockey.

I'm still trying to figure out where I'm going to play next. I may play at university. I'm pondering going back to school, which is a little daunting. I'm thirty-two, I've been away from university for ten years and I have a year and a half left in my Bachelor of Science degree. One option is to play with the Dinos at the University of Calgary. Another option is playing in the Western Women's Hockey League.

I might finish my degree and go into medicine. I see a lot of parallels between medicine and what we do in high performance sport—working with a team; solving problems; expectations and deadlines; pressure, with lots on the line. Maybe I'm a bit of an adrenalin junkie or addicted to difficult circumstances but challenge is part of my attraction to medicine. And ever since I was a kid I've enjoyed helping others. The problem with going to med school is that with playing hockey I've been away so much from my son. Medicine would be another intense pursuit. Can I afford that kind of time?

AM I HAPPY IT'S ALL OVER? Well, happy isn't the right word. The right word is relieved. I'm happy for our team, and for Canada, that we won. I'm relieved it's over. I'm just trying to enjoy some downtime for a while.

Part of that downtime means doing more things with Noah. Funny—when we toured Universal Studios we went on some of the rides and then took a backstage studio tour. He said, "You know, Mom, this is really what I came for, this backstage tour." He's ten years old, you'd think he'd love the rides, but he enjoyed looking at all the props and set designs.

On our vacation he was the safekeeper of my medal—it set off the security scanners at JFK Airport. Noah opened up the case to show the guard, who said, "What's this?" And Noah said, "That's my mom's Olympic medal!" He finds it cool when he can show it off to others, but he never says very much about it to me.

Here, I'll ask him:

"Noah Alexander, what did you like about the Olympics in Vancouver?"

"Ummm, sitting with the big Quatchi and Sumi and Miga... and Mukmuk. And walking around Robson Square. And I liked the opening ceremonies... And I liked being on the ice."

"You did? Were you nervous, watching your Mom play in the gold medal game?"

"No!"

"Did you think Mom's team was going to win?"

"Yeah, of course."

"Why do you think people want to be Olympic athletes, or go see an Olympics?"

"Well, it's a very big event. A big competition."

"Is there anything special about the Olympics?"

"You get to meet other people from the world? And you get to make friends with some other people from the world."

"Remember a while ago, when you said you thought hockey was boring. Do you still think it's boring?"

"Yeah."

"Okay, tell me something that you think isn't boring."

"Skiing. And Lego."

"What about the Russia Olympics in 2014? Do you think Mom should play there?"

"Yeah! Because I want to go there and see what it's like."

"You don't care about the hockey part, you just want to see Russia?"

"Yeah, I want to see Russia, but I'd like to see what the Olympics are like there."

"Do you think winning a gold medal is difficult?"

"Yeah, of course it is."

"What do you have to do to win one?"

"Train. Lift weights. Practise."

"So, if someone asked you: 'What does your Mom do for a living?' What would you tell them?"

"I would say she wins big medals. She plays hockey."

"And what do you want to do when you get older?"

"I want to work with the people at Lego Star Wars and create a new kind of Lego."

"Is that your passion? Do you think it's important for everyone to have a passion in life?"

"Yeah. They need to have something that they love."

"If you had a chance to compete in the Olympics which sport would you choose?"

"I would do bobsled or figure skating. Solo figure skating."

"I think you'd be a very good figure skater."

"Yeah, I'd do all the quads."

"In general, how would you describe yourself, Mr. Pacina?"

"I'm Cool. Diabolical. And Discombobulated."

"Your new favourite word! In closing, tell me what you think about this diary I've been keeping all year long. Do you think people will read it?"

"You've been doing it *all year* long?"

"How much is this interview going to cost me? A Lego piece?"

"A Lego set!"

Regardless of what the future holds, I can always count on Noah to help me keep things in perspective. At the end of the day, after all the gold medals and championships and hoopla, I'm still Boring Old Mom. And that's just fine with me.

Hayley Wickenheiser
GOLD MEDALLIST AND CAPTAIN,
2010 Canadian Olympic Women's Hockey Team

HAYLEY WICKENHEISER—captain of Canada's gold-medal-winning women's hockey team—has earned four Olympic and eight World Cup medals, and has been named her team's Most Valuable Player at two Olympics. A sixteen-year veteran of Canada's national team, Wickenheiser has more goals, assists, and penalties in international competition than any other woman; in 2010 she broke her team's Olympic scoring record. A determined player with a lethal slapshot, Wickenheiser has played professionally on men's teams in Sweden and Finland and also played softball for Canada in the 2000 Summer Olympics. In 2008 *Sports Illustrated* magazine included her on a list of the Top 25 Toughest Athletes in the World.

Wickenheiser's passion for hockey is matched by her drive to give back to the community through organizations such as KidSport, Dreams Take Flight, and Right to Play. She has led projects to raise the profile of women's hockey around the world and is a mentor for young athletes. She is working towards a Bachelor of Science degree at the University of Calgary.

WENDY LONG is a freelance writer specializing in sport-related stories. Since 2002 she has written for *TIME Canada*, 2010 Legacies Now, Ski Racing Canada, *Track and Field News*, Athletics Canada, the Canadian Olympic Committee, the True Sport Secretariat, PacificSport, UBC Department of Athletics, and the Canada's Sport Hall of Fame. From 1980 to 2002 she was a reporter with the *Vancouver Sun*, and in 1985 she became that paper's amateur sport and Olympic writer. She has covered seven Olympic Games, as well as Commonwealth, Pan-American, Goodwill, and Canada Games, World Cup skiing circuits, and World Track and Field Championships. She is the author of the book *Celebrating Excellence: Canadian Women Athletes*.